ORIENTATIONS

Kevin Nichols

ORIENTATIONS

Six Essays on
Theology and Education

1979

M.F.

St Paul Publications

St Paul Publications
Middlegreen, Slough SL3 6BT

Copyright © St Paul Publications 1979

Nihil obstat: **M. J. Byrnes**, ssp stl
Imprimatur: **F.** Diamond, vg, Northampton

Published **September** 1979

ISBN 085439 161 4

*St Paul Publications is an activity of the
priests and brothers of the Society of St Paul
who promote the christian message
through the mass media.*

To the Principals, staff and students
past and present
of Christ's College, Liverpool
with love and gratitude

Contents

Foreword

These essays have all been written while I have been preparing *Guidelines for Religious Education*. They are elaborations, in a rather more detailed and academic way, of some of the principal themes of *Guidelines*. So they may serve both to develop and to highlight these ideas. So also, although the chapters do not follow each other in any strict logical order, the book has, I hope, an inner, thematic unity.

Catechesis is a complex business; the more so since it must envisage several different levels. It is an initiation into the life and belief of the church community. But along with the church community it must look to the wider world both as context and as arena for mission. It is a traditional process, concerned with handing on the heritage of Catholic faith. Yet within the development of the Church's life it is not passive. It has a creative and dynamic function, eyes on the future as well as on the past. It has to communicate a type. But within that type it has to allow for and to promote personal growth. In this country at least, it is inextricably tangled with general educational developments and ideas. Hence the varied yet connected questions which seem to me at present the most prominent catechetical problems: the logical and practical relationship between catechesis and education; the relation of catechesis to the Church's mission and to its continuity; the basis of classroom religion; the catechetical connection between religion and morality; the idea of educational neutrality; the tensions present within the christian ideal of adulthood.

9

Most of these essays have been published before. "Religious Education: Mission and Maintenance" appeared in the *Clergy Review*, "Religion as a Classroom Subject" in *The Way*, "The Education of Conscience" in *Catholic Education Today*, "Religion and Counselling" in the *Bulletin* of the Catholic Marriage Advisory Council. I am grateful to the editors of these journals for permission to reprint them here. I am also grateful to Miss Iris Murdoch and Messrs Chatto & Windus for permission to print an extract from *The Nice and the Good*: to Professor Liam Hudson and Messrs Routledge and Kegan Paul for an extract from *Who are the Progressives Now?*: to Mr Robert Bolt and Messrs Samuel French for an extract from *A Man for All Seasons*.

I hope that these essays may make some small contribution to a continuing debate. But beyond that I hope they may help in our common pastoral and missionary task of centring and directing our catechetical work on principles which are evangelical, logically coherent and realistic. Catechesis cannot go forward without a firm centre. With one it can afford to make bold and radical initiatives. "He who is very firm at the centre can afford to be very free at the periphery". Behind the ideas and sustaining them, Christ himself is our real centre, our true orientation.

Ecce vir Oriens
nomen eius

1

Catechesis and Education

Whether or not Henry Ford really said "history is bunk", many people seem to believe it. Our ways of thinking about life are mostly oriented towards the future. What occurred and was said in the past seems based on naïve ignorance, an absence of refinement, a lack of accurate self-awareness. The future seems to offer the hope of richer life, of knowledgeable and responsible management of the cosmos. Our thinking about theology and catechesis is inevitably affected by this. A good deal of theology concerns itself with social problems and political movements. Some of it is influenced by that most future-oriented of all philosophies, Marxism. In catechetics too, we often ask ourselves questions like: "What kind of religious education will prepare children for life in the twenty-first century?" It is a real and important question. But the answer is not to be found entirely in the discernment of present trends nor in educated guesswork about future developments.

Even amateurs in theology cannot fail to notice the growth of another very different kind of approach. It is the return to a concentration of interest on the scriptures and the life of the early Church. We speak more often of the gospel and the kingdom than we do of doctrines or the Church. There is a tendency to look at doctrinal statements, moral principles and liturgical practices in a historical perspective so that they can be seen as part of the changing and developing life of the Church. More than that, there is a tendency to overlook the intervening centuries and find the most significant lessons of history in the earliest christian days. This can be carried too far. You cannot put the clock back. You cannot return to primitive Christianity. It would not be possible, nor would it be right. For the mission of the Church is to speak God's word to the age in which it finds itself. The necessary adaptations are governed by the principle of development and the guidance of the magisterium. Nevertheless, there is a sense in which the scriptural and patristic age of the Church is normative. It is the original and most crucial embodiment of God's word in human thought and human affairs. Thought which bases itself there is radical in the sense that it is a return to roots. Western philosophy, it has been said, is a series of footnotes to Plato. Christian theology is, in a similar sense, a series of footnotes to the New Testament.

The word "catechesis" itself has been resurrected from the Church's early days. Then it was common. In more recent times it has fallen into disuse. Although it is neither a familiar nor a particularly beautiful word, I believe that we ought to try to bring it back into common use. I believe that this would help to clarify and solve some of the tangled issues which beset our discussions about religious education. In the early Church, catechesis was certainly not education. Even by the criteria of the time, it was something else. In the early days, the Church lived in a state of diaspora. It consisted of a number of small groups scattered like seeds among the pagan nations, cells, growing in size but existing in a non-christian world. Christians, therefore, were instinctively inward-looking, concerned about establishing and maintaining their own identity. Inarticulate consciousness of that was one of the factors which led them to give so much time and attention to the initiation of new members. They insisted on a long and demanding catechumenate. To be a catechumen was a recognised form of christian existence. The catechumen had acknowledged Christ. He had made an act of faith and asked for admission to the sacraments. He prepared for this by receiving instruction and by participating in the liturgy of the word. His progress was periodically scrutinised by the church community. Only with their consent could he eventually receive the sacraments of initiation during the Easter Vigil. The image of "gestation" used in that vigil catches the feel of the whole process. It contained elements of instruction and examination. But essentially it was a long organic, many-sided process of growth with a strong liturgical framework.

All those who belonged to the catechumenate were adults. The point of departure for a catechumen was a decision to accept the Lord's word and to ask for baptism. Only an adult could make this choice. But children could not be entirely left out. Sometimes fathers would carry their children with them when they joined the catechumenate or when they came to be baptised. So these children became members of the Church not through the regular process of initiation but by the principle of family solidarity. The catechesis of children of christian families, their true initiation into conscious christian life would have to come later.

After the conversion of Constantine, the character of church life changed radically. It was now no longer a private group. It was the official religion of imperial Rome. Membership of it ceased to be a matter of personal choice. It became increasingly a part of the established social order. The questions: "What is it to be a Christian?" and "How does a person become one?" began to appear in a new light. *Three profound changes in the formation of Christians followed on this event and the consequences of them are still with us. The first* was the occurrence, in a number of european countries, of mass baptisms. The catechumens were no longer a few persons who could be known individually. They numbered thousands — a king and his barons, the whole population of a locality. Missionaries faced with this situation could give no more than a very sketchy catechesis. There could be no long period of preparation, little instruction, no personal scrutiny. So gradually,

13

all the characteristics of the catechumenate, as it had been known to the early Church, disappeared.

The second change was the gradual shift in emphasis from adults to children. Once Christianity had become a part of social life — indeed its basis — initiation into the christian faith was no longer an option. The question now was no longer one of choice but one of upbringing. Catechesis — such as it was — became a part of the process of socialisation. No longer did those responsible ask: How do you prepare adults who want to be Christians for baptism? They asked — though probably not very consciously — How do you initiate children into the values and beliefs which the adult world holds?

This decay of the idea of catechesis led to the *third change*, the one with which we are here most directly concerned. It is the involvement of the Church with the processes of formal education and the gradual absorption of the idea of catechesis into these. Confrontations between the Church and education occurred quite early for the Church could scarcely avoid taking some kind of stand in relation to the Greek philosophical schools. But it was a cautious and a controversial one, for many thought that the wisdom of the word had nothing to gain from human learning. Indeed some thought that the glorious gospel would always be in conflict with human philosophy; Quid Athenae Hierosolymis? But others saw that christian faith could no longer be private and esoteric. It must stand up for itself in the intellectual market-place of the world. By the third century, Origen was "instructing catechumens of superior intelligence into the philosophical disciplines". The school of Alexandria was rejecting the idea of Christianity as an arcane mystery religion and asserting the unity of truth. There is, wrote Clement, "one river of truth and many streams fall into it from this side and that".

In for a penny, in for a pound. From a cautious "ostpolitik", the Church's involvement in general education became first one of whole-hearted commitment, then one of dominance and control. During the Dark Ages, only the

14

Church preserved and transmitted what remained of the classical heritage. During the Middle Ages it achieved a new and brilliant synthesis of classical philosophy and the truths of revelation. This synthesis was the basis of an educational curriculum, the liberal arts, philosophy and theology, which became universal in western Europe. From initiation into private and distinctively religious mysteries to induction into a comprehensive and integrated world-view; from catechesis to education. This was the approach which, adapted in various ways, held the field for several centuries; though it was an educational scheme which reached only a small number of people.

J.H. Newman's lectures "On the Scope and Nature of University Education" is a classical exposition of this view. For Newman, theology has a rightful place in education. Indeed it is the keystone of the whole structure. But it must not trespass on other fields. Liberal education especially has its own nobility and its own inherent value. Liberal knowledge is not learning, not the amassing of facts, nor, except indirectly, is it professional training. Its aim is to develop the "philosophic habit", a beauty of the mind, the ability to order and judge intelligently and sensitively. It brings a grace to every particular task. It develops natural qualities which may serve the life of faith. They *may* serve it. There is a certain hesitancy, an ambiguity in Newman's great book. On the one hand it is a celebration of intellect. On the other hand, he realises that it may lead to an elegant parody of religion; which is no more than human excellence unsavoured by the salt of humility; whose devotees become "the victims of their own intense self-contemplation".

Newman acknowledges — though he would not have used these terms — that integral humanism is not always the servant of the gospel; that there is a certain conflict between education and catechesis. Liberal education may make people self-centredly clever. It may make them so logically critical as not to be open to the mysteries of the spirit.

Newman's hesitation points ahead to one of the reasons why, in due course, the long alliance between the Church and education began to weaken. Thoughtful catechists began to perceive that in being reduced to an educational form, catechesis had lost its rich diversity and some of its power. After the industrial revolution mass education began to be introduced throughout Europe. The form it took was a far cry from say the humanist schools of Vittorio da Feltre and the christian educators of the Renaissance. It concentrated on basic knowledge and basic skills taught in a mechanical way. Such methods applied to religion could hardly hope to provide an adequate initiation into the mysteries of the faith. So a movement began to revive the scriptural-liturgical catechesis of ancient days. It was to be kerygmatic — more concerned about speaking the word of faith with power than with doctrinal instruction. It was to be linked closely with the life of the christian community of faith. It was hard — though not altogether impossible — to envisage such a process going on within the framework of a nineteenth century elementary school.

Other non-religious factors contributed to this loosening of the ties between catechesis and education. One was the growth of secular states and the general secularisation of Europe. This gave birth to a secular idea of education based on technical and social competence; or on an idea of liberal education for its own sake. Newman's fear of a culture and an education based on an ideal of liberal knowledge unchecked by the discipline of theology began to be realised. It found little place for religion, certainly not as the unifying element in knowledge, the keystone of the house of intellect. Later a more sophisticated idea of education appeared. This was the concept of an initiation into the various fields of human knowledge and experience. It aims at developing rational autonomy in these fields according to their different natures. It certainly allows religion a place, but chiefly as a field within which critical reflection can be deployed. Children can learn about religion, they can even be helped to develop a sympathetic insight into it. But the concept is entirely at odds with the idea of an initiation into mysteries or the handing on of a heritage of faith. So catechesis is a square peg in this educational hole; though, as I shall argue later, there has recently been some *rapprochement* between the two and it may be that this will increase.

These changes in the idea of education emerged from a changing society. Increasingly, western society became secular. It was no longer based on substantial beliefs commonly held. It became open, diverse, pluralist. Values and beliefs were no longer to be imposed or socially supported. It became much more like the world in which the Church had first grown up. Popular education developed in a world which was still notionally christian and offered a basic preparation for life in that society. No doubt, while Christianity remained established in public life, basic religious instruction was frequently sufficient to ensure perseverance in christian belief and practice. But in a world where the mass media brought vividly home to children the diversity of beliefs, it began to prove ineffective. Realisation of this strengthened the case of those who thought that the fusing of catechesis and education had been a mistaken course. The question was raised: What kind of preparation will help christian faith to thrive at the end of the twentieth century? The answer began to be given less in terms of formal education, more in the ancient language of catechesis. A reflective, well-rooted faith based on strong personal commitment seemed to be what was needed. Formal education seemed unlikely to develop that.

From these changes and from the reflections of those who grappled with them, was born a revival of the idea of a catechumenate. It seems theologically sound because it aims at the "free adherence to God in faith" which the General Catechetical Directory proposes as the true aim of catechesis; because it deals directly with the mysteries of faith; because it is closely linked with the Church as community; because it has a strong liturgical framework; because its many-sided approach to initiation reflects the

17

complexity of the mature act of faith in human beings. It seems socially necessary because of the cultural situation in which Christians today find themselves. The Synod of 1977 teaches that the adult catechumenate should be the model towards which all other forms of catechetical work should look. The new *Rite for the christian initiation of adults* embodies the same point. Its principle is that only adults can freely ask for it and free choice is its necessary condition. The *Rite* is one among several influences which is shifting the emphasis in catechetical work from children back to adults. We need to consider the implications of this rather dramatic shift and of the revived catechumenate for our own policy and practice.

The adult catechumenate is proposed to us as a model, not as a universal formula. It is a norm towards which we look and must therefore be adapted. There are other, perfectly valid forms of catechesis. The principal one is the catechesis of children. How are we to understand this in the perspective of the catechumenate? Two points are important in answering this question and making this adaptation. *In the first place,* the catechumenate was a climactic process leading up to Easter baptism and it began in the free choice of an adult. Nowadays most people come to catechesis already baptised and they come to it as children so that these two factors must be missing. But they are not the only constitutive elements of a catechumenate. It can still be a gradual many-sided process of growth in faith rather than a presentation of all its mysteries to be swallowed in one gulp. It can be made the business of the whole church community. It can involve family and friends, parish and school in such a way that growth in faith is not restricted to one segment of life nor limited to one kind of learning. It can be punctuated — indeed consecrated — by regular liturgical celebrations. It can include instruction, discussion, participation, action, experience, relationships. It can, in this way, look towards the development of a faith which is free, thoughtful and rich while accepting children as they are with their various

18

limitations. *Secondly*, it should not concentrate too much on children's limitations but should pay attention also to their strengths. Children are not pre-religious nor pre-christian. They have qualities which give to the religious life of childhood its own distinctive character and value. Children have a sense of wonder, a trustful dependence, a capacity for direct and spontaneous relationships. All of these are components of a mature adult faith. The task of a catechist of children is to nourish them, not to kill them off in favour of a rational, self-conscious construct which embodies the worst aspects of contemporary adulthood.

Most of us are baptised as infants. Adult catechesis, nowadays, cannot therefore have the quality of building up towards baptism. Yet it too should be oriented towards the catechumenate and should have the many-sided character which that requires. It may with advantage have some climax other than baptism. It would be invaluable if we could devise a proper, well-constructed catechumenate for those preparing for marriage; or for those who will be commissioned to some form of pastoral or liturgical ministry; or indeed for those who are terminally ill.

So far in this essay I have been concerned mainly to present an "idea" — as Newman would have used that word — of catechesis. The catechetical process is diverse, it adapts, it happens in different settings and takes account of different circumstances. But it is unified because all its various forms "home" in different ways on the adult catechumenate. One of its forms is the educational one. This — catechesis as part of the process of schooling — is probably the most familiar to us; certainly it is the form into which we have put most of our resources. Some argue that schooling is wholly at odds with the idea of a catechumenate. They call for a drastic change — the de-schooling of our catechetical practice. This, I think, is a responsible challenge and one to be taken seriously. I turn now and finally to consider the question: Is a catechumenate possible within the setting of formal education? Is catechesis reconcileable with education?

The case I wish to argue is this; first that the Church should be involved in education for its own sake; secondly that catechesis can take an acceptable and valuable educational form. The first point need not detain us long. Most people would agree with the principle. One aspect of the Church's mission — not the whole of it, not the only dimension of it — is the betterment of human life. Man's supernatural destiny is not wholly separable from his human progress, nor human values from the values of the gospel. The Church may undertake educational work in much the same way and for much the same reasons as it undertakes the care of the sick. Moreover, education is a task so permeated with values that the Church has its own unique and distinctive contribution to make.

The second point in this case is more contentious. For many argue for the total banishment of catechetical elements from education. It should, they think, be non-confessional. Plainly, catechesis can never be that, for the confession of faith is not only its purpose but its starting-point. Yet education has changed since the days when its aim was to provide basic skills for the children of the new urban proletariat. It is concerned now with the education of feeling and with moral education as well as with knowledge and useful skills. It is concerned with the quality of the educational community as well as with classroom teaching and the curriculum. It has a pastoral dimension. It is concerned about the relationship between the school and the local community. All of this represents a certain "apertura". It allows some elbow-room, broadens the scope of education so that at least some elements of catechesis can find a place in it. So in a church school, the quality of relationships and pastoral care, the school community and its liturgy represent elements of a catechesis.

Religion as a classroom subject is the field in which the protagonists of "pure education" make their most uncompromising stand. Yet here again there is some convergence. Catechists cannot accept the non-confessional principle. But there are other aspects of this position with which they could hardly quarrel. Education aims, among other things, to make religious faith more thoughtful, to make commitment more critical, reflective and better-informed. Catechists also aim at these things; the "free adherence to God in faith" of the General Catechetical Directory translates very readily into an educational register. These aims of course do not represent the full scope of the catechist's task. He will be concerned with the essence of faith, as well as its development. He will try to find ways of making the experience of faith — which he himself is inside — accessible to children. He will lead worship not with the aim of sympathetic insight but as a substantive and formative act. He will work within a tradition of faith and be concerned with handing on its heritage; a tradition is a living and growing thing; it does not involve blind learning of a static body of stuff. It is therefore an ambient within which real education can happen. Yet, in so far as he is working in the setting of formal education, the catechist will cut his coat to suit his cloth. He will concentrate his attention on those aspects of catechesis which can reasonably be called "educational" — understanding, thoughtfulness, reflective experience. This is the basis for the claim that there is a mode or style of catechesis which can legitimately be called educational.[1]

If this argument is sound its consequences for our catechetical policy are these. To have and to maintain a system of church schools, along the lines set out here, is to have a great asset. This is a purely theoretical statement based on the certainty that our Catholic schools have served the church community well in the past and a conviction that they can do the same in the future. Some aspects of that conviction can and should be tested empirically. It is possible to enquire into the present performance of our church schools measured against catechetical criteria.

---

[1] I have argued this point at greater length in *Cornerstone*, chapters 2 and 8 (St Paul Publications, 1978).

We could monitor the progress of experiments to see which aspects of schooling offer the greatest catechetical promise. But the results of these enquiries would always be ambiguous. They could be used equally by those who wish to abolish Catholic schools and those who wish to improve them. The latter form a large majority. They express, as Newman might have said, a common certitude within which investigations take place. The right policy is to act on this certitude unless it can be shown that catechesis is altogether at odds with schooling. This, I have argued, is not the case.

The danger of massive schooling, however, is that to commit all our resources — of money, persons and energy — to this large and expensive enterprise, is to concentrate attention on certain aspects of catechetical work and to exclude others. Our policy should be to develop our schools along catechetical lines within the limits set out in the previous paragraphs. Beyond that, we should develop other complementary forms of catechesis outside the educational setting. This we should do, not as though we were indulging in an optional extra or supporting a poor relation. We should undertake it as a major part of the mission of the Church. In this way, we may hope to realise on several fronts and in various ways the ideal of catechesis as ministry of the Word.

2

Religious Education:
Mission and Maintenance

I have borrowed the words "mission" and "maintenance" from the title of a book by Michael Winter. It is not my direct intention to discuss the thesis of that book which argues for a radical overhaul of the pastoral structures of our Church in terms of the concept of "mission". However, since the two words have already become something of a theological adage, I thought that it would be worthwhile to explore the concepts they represent and to attempt some application of them to policy and practice in religious education. I think it is important, first of all, to unpack the concepts a little since neither is a simple idea. For one thing, the word "mission" has an aura of theological glamour, whereas "maintenance" which we associate largely with sparking plugs and blocked drains, seems prosaic, if not slightly squalid. "Mission" is a hurrah-word. "Maintenance" is a boo-word. It is important for clarity, for accuracy, even for responsibility, to prise away the inherent associations in order to inspect the real content of the ideas.

"Mission" seems ordinarily to mean the bringing to others of some valued state of affairs. We ought to look more closely at the two elements in this definition. The first is the act of bringing to others. It involves the activities of spreading and propagating, of changing and converting others. It entails that the valued state of affairs is not regarded as a personal possession to be hoarded, but as something which ought to be communicated as widely as possible. It is true, therefore, that missionaries are outward-looking people: if that is taken to mean that they give more of their attention and concern to those who do not possess the missionary object than to those who do. Indeed they may well give more attention to others than to the missionary object itself. Neither history nor contemporary experience lacks instances of people with a mission whose object is vague, even to themselves — perhaps the betterment of the human lot or the improvement of our race. Such free-floating missionary zeal is rarely serious. When it is, it can be a disruptive and destructive force. Lacking an object correlative it easily becomes loose energy floating on the surface of life and attaching itself to whatever cause is most topical or most readily to hand.

This consideration leads directly into the second element in my definition, the missionary object, the valued state of affairs itself. In the first place we can say that the object is not only valued but is in itself valuable — in the sense of having seriously to do with important values and not with trivialities. It is true that we could not rule it out logically that a person should have a mission about stamp-collecting or the preservation of Victorian pillar-boxes. But we can say that he would be given the title "missionary" only by courtesy or with the tongue in the cheek. To use the word in its mainstream of meaning we rightly require reasonable precision in the object and also that it be connected with a serious value-question.

Two other considerations may serve as corollaries since they seem loosely connected with this element in the definition. The first is that there is a certain consonance between mission and simplicity. It is true that there is no logical necessity for the missionary object to be either simple or complex. Nevertheless, when we reflect on history and experience, it seems that mission is usually connected with some simple truth, insight or moral principle, rather than with a complex intellectual or moral system. It is easier to spread and propagate personal evangelical piety than institutional Catholicism with its superstructure of theological, moral and administrative systems. It is easier to preach the simple ideal of equality than to recommend a social order based on complex financial, economic and political balances. To say that it is easier does not of course entail that it is better. To say that would be to give an unreasonable advantage to over-simplifiers. Nietzsche once remarked that the Lutheran Reformation was the revolt of the simple against the complex.

The second tentative corollary is that missionary objects tend to adapt as circumstances and cultures require. It is true that mission sometimes has a very rigid and inflexible object like that of Calvin's Geneva or the religion of the Mennonite sect in the United States. But these tend to be short-lived. A missionary object which is to last needs the ability to adapt to circumstances without losing its identity.

I will define "maintenance" as the preservation of a valued state of affairs so that it continues to fulfil its function. We do not therefore connect with the concept dynamic and active words like "spreading" or "propagating". Maintenance is inward-looking in so far as it devotes more of its attention to its object than to those who do not possess or share it. The maintainer does not take kindly to changes in the valued object, which therefore does not show the same tendency to adapt as does the missionary object. However, maintenance is an idea which connects more easily with complex objects than with simple ones. Perhaps this is because complex states of affairs have an intrinsic fascination. Perhaps it is because simple objects take so little looking after.

However, I have added another and important element to the definition. This is that maintenance is undertaken in view of the object's function. We do not speak seriously of maintaining a car unless it is intended to go. Nor is a house maintained except to be lived in, or at least to be looked at and admired. The functional element makes a considerable difference to the concept of maintenance. For if the object being maintained is the Lord's gospel as it comes to us in church tradition; and if the function of this object includes its being preached to all nations; then the maintainer as well as the missionary will have his attention directed to those who do not share the same object.

I should now like to consider what I will call the missionary thesis. It is a thesis which argues that the structures of our Church are an example of the concept of maintenance. They have grown up in a variety of historical circumstances and bear the marks of their historical origins. They are preserved not because they are of value or importance but simply from instinctive conservative instincts. They affect the life and work of the Church deeply and they are now a hindrance to the spreading of the gospel. They should be scrapped and replaced by structures devised in the light of the new knowledge about individual and group life available in the human sciences.

There are three objections to this thesis which I shall now raise and discuss. The first is the question: In our faith what is a structure? Anyone who has attempted, or even listened to, hermeneutics, the work of detaching "essential meaning" from historical and cultural expression, is aware of the great difficulty and delicacy of the task. This is true when one tries to precipitate out the essential message of scripture from its literary forms. It is also true of the effort to express the permanent essence of a doctrinal statement, freed from its temporary, time-conditioned, philosophical colouring. It is true also, when one tries to say whether a moral rule or principle is of the essence of christian morality, and how far it is due to a mistaken understanding of moral facts — for instance of economic matters or of human psychology.

It is true, even though less obviously so, in matters of church order. It seems to me that the differences here are of degree rather than of kind. At either extreme, there are probably statements or principles we could be sure about. Everyone would agree that, say, the wearing of clerical dress is a marginal and time-conditioned practice. Everyone would agree that loving our neighbour is a permanent and inescapable christian duty. But in between the two, there is a very large area in which it is very difficult to analyse and make distinctions. Everyone knows that the Holy Office is a structure. But what about the Holy Eucharist? It, like every other expression of our faith is marked by the historical conditions of its origin and developments. Sometimes essence and accidents seem to be inextricably mingled. The question remains: which is the baby and which the bath-water? Which can go down the plug-hole and which is necessary for the continuity of life?

It may be answered to this objection that the difficulty and delicacy of a task makes it more not less necessary that it should be undertaken; that the work of theology is precisely to make these distinctions and that this work should be intensified. I agree with this reply, but not with some of its consequences. For, given that the work is of great difficulty and complexity; and given that the answers proposed are many and diverse and some of them highly speculative; then it does not seem right to speak of radical root-and-branch reforms on the basis of a body of evidence so fragile and so incomplete.

The second objection is connected with the first. It is that in our Church, there is, besides the principle of development and change, the principle of identity and continuity. The Church's historical pilgrimage not only lends various cultural colourings to our faith. It also provides ways in which new facets of that faith are progressively discovered and articulated through the clash of faith and culture, gospel and philosophy. The christian idea, as Newman wrote, may sometimes take false trails or follow blind alleys. But the principle of its life is a developmental one, a principle of cumulative growth. Consequently the structures which history has produced are more than accidental episodes. They may contain elements which need to be altered or

27

rejected. But they also contain a core of truth and value. The idea of a sudden, root-and-branch reform involves the risk of losing the principle of continuity and identity. It uses history to disown the past, and this is not, in religious matters, history's business. Moreover, we may view with some suspicion the intention of replacing the structures of the Church with a new set derived systematically and comprehensively from the human sciences. For those sciences themselves are in a state of becoming. They are subject to rapid changes and the degree of certainty, even the kind of knowledge they achieve, is unsure. They are no doubt, more self-conscious, more self-aware than history, but they are equally relative. Moreover, it is well known that the application of the methods of the human sciences to religious questions bristles with theoretical and practical problems and that the most profound of these remain unsolved.

The third objection is that the missionary thesis puts too much emphasis on the place of structures in church life. It is of course true at all levels that extremely tight, legalistic unyielding structures kill the spirit. But it is also true that people can work very well within structures which are somewhat unwieldy and out of date but moderately flexible. On the other hand, people who have to work within structures which are very slight or whose basis is uncertain, find themselves uneasy and insecure. Who has not come across a parish or a school or a liturgical development which has been re-vivified by an intelligent and zealous person; a person who has not overthrown the structures but has seen new possibilities for working within them? Although the two are inextricably connected, conversion of heart is both logically and psychologically prior to structural reform.

I base upon these objections the thesis which I now wish to put forward. It is the thesis that in the renewal of our Church — whether of its pastoral practice or its educational work — the concepts of mission and maintenance are of equal and complementary importance. The case for maintenance arises out of the considerations I have already advanced. In the course of its long history, Peter's barque has undoubtedly become encrusted with institutional barnacles. But if you prise these away, you will find a sound hull. There is no justification for constructing an entirely new ship. To do that, even supposing that some theological genius could comprehensively detach essence from accidents, would still be misconceived. For christian history is not an unfortunate accident to be written off. It represents a gradual growth in the understanding of our faith. To abandon tradition, as much as to abandon scripture, would be to destroy something essential to Christianity. It would be to risk losing the identity of christian faith and christian life. It would risk replacing it by a human construct whose value would depend entirely on the empirical evidence available for its support. Moreover, it is possible to adapt institutions and structures as well as radically replacing them. And adaptation seems to accord better with the view that our history is a process of gradual and cumulative evolution of christian understanding and living.

However, I am not advocating an idea of tradition as hanging grimly on to everything; as though devotion to the nine first Fridays and the doctrine of the Incarnation had equal traditional standing. The concept of mission certainly has its claims. A valued state must be maintained in view of its function. Where it is maintained purely for its own sake we have not a dynamic force but a museum-piece; not the saving and glorious gospel but ecclesiastical correctness. Where it can be shown plainly that some of our church structures impede that mission, then there must be changes, even major ones. But these changes must respect tradition, they must consciously try to grow out of it. They must not be based on a simplistic idea of the gospel nor on contemporary social ideals. They must not risk a major fracture in the historical development of our Church which remains its guarantee of organic identity with the mission and the teaching of Jesus.

In putting forward this view of the renewal of the life of our Church, I am advocating what Professor Karl Popper called piecemeal rather than utopian social engineering. I am suggesting that our church institutions and structures should be examined critically. But this critical revision should not only have an eye on their probable obsolescence. It should have an eye also on the probable worth and value that lies in them. They should be examined individually. It should not be assumed that what is true of one is true of all. If they can be conclusively shown to impede our Church's mission, then they should be discarded or adapted. But there is not available to us a new utopian blueprint derived from sociology and psychology which will solve all our institutional ills. To adopt one is to fall into the errors of Professor Popper's enemies of the open society — the utopian social engineers, Plato, Hegel and Marx.

Obviously church structures vary a great deal in the seriousness with which we should take them. The organisation of religious education is not, I suppose, one of the most central. Nevertheless, it is affected by the missionary thesis in two main ways, one bearing on the content of religious education and the other on the Church's educational policy.

First of all, mission requires that we direct our attention mainly to those who do not possess the valued state. Hence, religious education should concentrate its attention on the world around and beyond the Church. The Church's mission is to bring the gospel to that world and to serve it by promoting human values, by working for a juster social order, by contributing to the solution of the urgent problems of the day. Therefore, religious education should contain a great deal of material about that world and those problems. So, in this thesis, life-themes and comparative religion would be favoured more than scriptural or doctrinal material. Equally, since Christians must act independently in this world, the promotion of autonomy, independence of mind and a critical outlook in religious matters is recommended; at the expense of the submissive and accepting aspects of faith; at the expense perhaps of the truth that faith is essentially a denial of our own self-sufficiency.

This view of the content of religious education is open to many of the objections to the "missionary thesis" that I raised earlier. It risks failing to communicate what is essential in its anxiety to allow for changing cultural circumstances. It risks a breakdown in the historical continuity which guarantees the organic identity of christian teaching today with the gospel of Christ. It seems that the just claims of maintenance demand that apart from topicality and social relevance the authoritative contemporary expressions of Catholic faith be taught with reasonable precision and reasonable thoroughness. How this is to be done is certainly a problem. That it should be given up as impossible or impracticable is infinitely more disturbing.

At the other extreme to this is the classical "maintenance" thesis. This is that the content of religious education should consist entirely in the transmission of the existing status quo in the Church — only established doctrines, traditional moral rules, devotional practices and conventional ecclesiastical life. The weaknesses of this position are plain. It is likely to alienate because of its rigidity and irrelevance to modern life. Or where it takes, it is likely to produce Catholics of a very rigid outlook who will neither live well in the contemporary world, nor be of much use in the Church's mission to it. Still more seriously, it canonises a certain phase in the development of Catholic faith. It takes the post-Tridentine, Ultramontane era as the final, perfect, unalterable expression of Catholic truth. Undoubtedly, the authoritarian and rather repressive Catholicism of those centuries had its strengths. But from our present standpoint in history we can see that it was also marked by some extremely serious limitations and a few quite grotesque distortions.

I suggest that there is a third way between these two extreme positions. I will sum it up by saying that the aim of religious education in a church context is the initiation

31

of children into a living tradition of faith. In this account, the word tradition stands for the concept of maintenance. The word living indicates the dynamic and missionary quality that such an education should have. It is a difficult educational ideal. It is relatively simple to teach children a body of doctrinal propositions, if they are what Whitehead called inert ideas. It is even fairly straightforward to socialise children into a static subculture, the way our traditional parochial education often did. To initiate into a living tradition is difficult because the terms in the process will not stay still to be analysed. I will try nevertheless to be a little more specific about what this educational ideal entails.

It requires six factors. *First*, it requires knowledge of Catholic beliefs. *Secondly*, the learning must go beyond knowledge to understanding; and this demands some grasp of the history and development of the Catholic faith; and also awareness of the inner coherence of that faith, its shape, its architecture. *Thirdly*, this education should promote acceptance of these beliefs. You can, of course, lead a horse to the water; you can't make him drink. You cannot teach faith. But, as in the case of morality, there are teaching methods which indirectly promote it. *Fourthly*, these beliefs must be learned in a way which is relevant and meaningful; that is their application to the problems of personal and social life must be evident. *Fifthly*, this teaching should promote an active and apostolic religious outlook. Faith ought to appear not as a personal possession to be hoarded but as a source of responsibility to others and to our race. *Finally*, this initiation should promote, not only a sense of belonging to a community of faith, but also the sense of having an active and responsible part to play in the life of that community.

On the other hand, it would not be sufficient to constitute this ideal, if one were to say that the aim of religious education is to help children to take the religious dimension of life seriously. Nor would it be sufficient to construct a curriculum based on developing religious abilities; such

32

as the ability to think clearly about religious questions, to apply principles to concrete cases or to share sympathetically in religious experiences. Nor again would it be adequate to aim at promoting a deeper understanding of human experiences and their mysteriousness. These general religious factors will no doubt have a part in religious education in a church context. They may form a basis for the curriculum which meets educational criteria. But they do not do justice to theological considerations.

The other main way in which the "missionary thesis" affects religious education is the doubt it casts on the worth-whileness of separate church schools. Church schools, it is argued, create an inward-looking mentality. They separate Catholic children off from their fellows and concentrate their attention, religiously speaking, on the Church rather than on their mission to the world. Many people I suspect really wish that Catholic schools did these things a bit more effectively. Nevertheless, I would like to make one or two observations on this case.

The first is that this, like all of the other arguments against church schools, with two exceptions, lends itself equally well either to the conclusion that they should be abandoned or to the conclusion that they should be improved. The two exceptions are the argument from social divisiveness and the argument from indoctrination. In the first case, it must be admitted that there may well be some circumstances in which separate church schools perpetuate social discord to an extent that makes them indefensible. But these circumstances are not common, and it is hard to see them realised in this country at all. In the case of the second argument, the concept of indoctrination is a notoriously slippery customer: of the many senses in which it is used, it is hard to see which applies to church schools with any logical necessity.

These questions apart, the general thesis I have been arguing lends at least a probability to the conclusion that our church schools should be kept and improved. Their basis in the contemporary world — certainly different from that put forward in 1870 or 1902 — needs to be re-formulated in the light of theological change (including the theology of mission); and in the light of the character, hopes and problems of contemporary society. We have in this country, a dual system which obliges our schools to be both a part of the Church and a part of our national educational enterprise. It is a situation which, in theory at least, lends itself ideally to the marriage of maintenance and mission. To work it out in practice is, of course, as in many marriages, another and more difficult matter. But it is a hope well worth pursuing.

3

Religion as a Classroom Subject

To put it that way: "Religion as a classroom subject" sounds a bit odd; not only unusual, but logically odd as well. For we are apt to think of religion in universal and absolute terms, as a reality "caught not taught" which cannot be confined in a strait-jacket of chalk and talk, lesson-notes, timetables, syllabuses and curriculum-planning. Harold Loukes wrote of the content of religious education as the "depth of realisation of everything, the experience of the whole, the living and the human". And, lest we should imagine that only liberal Protestants think this way, let us set beside his words, those from the General Catechetical Directory:

> For every man whose mind is open to the message of the gospel, catechesis is a particularly apt means for him to understand God's plan in his own life and to examine the highest meaning of existence and history, so that the life of individual men and of society may be illumined by the light of the kingdom of God and be conformed to its demands, and the mystery of the Church as the community of those who believe in the gospel may be able to be recognised (§21).

These olympian ideas are difficult to wing and bring to earth. Yet, if religion is to be taught in the classroom, it has to submit to those limitations and structures which make class-teaching possible. The phrase "religion as an occupation" is a similar case. It strikes an odd and jarring note. Yet if some people are to spend all their time on religious matters, then professional considerations, job-satisfaction, salaries and pensions must count for something as well as liturgy and divine providence.

A century ago, this logical oddness did not exist. Religion appeared then, as an established body of knowledge which stood alongside other established disciplines and formed the basis of the curriculum. So, Newman could discuss theology in relation to other subjects as the basis of a unified educational programme. But now religion is a rather shadowy presence in the intellectual market-place. Moreover, many would argue that the basis of its place in the curriculum is not religious knowledge or even understanding. They would say that it is "appreciating religious experience" or "making a free and informed commitment" or "developing a mature faith". A different "model" of the curriculum is being used. It is not based on an established house of intellect with different areas of knowledge related to each other in a simple framework. It looks rather to individual and social needs. It does not assume that educational purposes will follow the pattern of organised academic knowledge. A secure lodgement for religion in this curriculum structure is much more difficult to find.

It is my contention that, in recent developments in religious education, too many large abstract words, too many high-level vague ideas have been used without their meaning being clearly defined or their implications worked out. Examples are the word "kerygma", the word "relationship" and the word "experience". I do not doubt that these words represent valid and important ideas. But I think that they have not been pursued systematically into the content, methods and structures of the religious curriculum. There has been an absence of lower-range questions, like: Is it possible or desirable to preach the Lord's kerygma in the classroom?: What kinds of teaching are likely to promote relationships?: Are all experiences of equal worth or do they come in different kinds? Consequently, there is a poor logical connection between these large, rather vague ideas and the reality of the textbook and the classroom. Where there is a lack of connection between aims and actualities there develops the lack of a sense of purpose; as a faulty connection brings electric current to the bulb only in fitful bursts.

I hope in this paper to make a little progress with the question: What is the status of religious education in the school curriculum? and given that this can be answered with some clarity, with the logically consequent question: What are the aims? I hope to avoid the subtleties and the jargon of the recently and rapidly developed body of curriculum theory. That theory nonetheless is the framework within which I am working. It requires that the aims of the curriculum be thought out in a broadly philosophical way; yet in a form definite enough for the aims to be teased out into more specific objectives. These need not be strictly behavioural but they must be concrete enough to guide the construction of curricular material and to direct that construction. The first question then, is that of justification: *What is the case for religion in school education?* The second question is one of taxonomy: *Can its place be systematically worked out in terms of the curriculum?*

I turn then, to the first question which, put simply is: Is religious education possible? I do not mean, of course, is it possible as a matter of empirical fact. There is a story of an American revivalist preacher who leaned over a fence and asked an old negro hoeing the cotton: "Brother, do you believe in baptism?" "Why sure I believe in baptism" came the reply, "I've seen it done". We have all seen religious education done. Or at least we have seen something which we would describe as religious education going on. My question rather is the logical one: Can we show that religious education is not a contradiction in terms? Can we give an account of religion and of education to show that the two are not logically incompatible? For some would

37

argue that while religion can rightly be connected with training or even with socialisation, education is a process with which it is not compatible unless it is treated objectively — as in comparative religion or the history of the Church.

Let us examine the two concepts and try to see whether this is so. I am content for the moment, to accept the established view of education proposed by R.S. Peters, Paul Hirst and others in a number of books. According to this view, an activity, if it is to count as education, must meet three criteria. *First* it must be an initiation into some worthwhile area of knowledge or experience. Worthwhileness is the most difficult factor to account for. Maybe it must depend upon a common and perhaps a temporary view of life. At present we would say that it would allow science and music, but exclude necromancy and shove halfpenny. *Secondly,* the activity must be set in a rational tradition. It must include reason and reasonableness in some way even though it is not essentially an intellectual activity. So we would have to exclude behavioural therapy and track-training on the grounds that they are mechanical or unconscious. *Thirdly,* it must promote independence of mind. Conditioning or indoctrination would not meet this criteria because they both try, in different ways, to set up patterns of behaviour which will be proof against critical thought. Which account of religion, if any, will meet these three criteria?

Before I discuss two or three recent accounts, I note the striking fact that accounts given from *within* religion are especially difficult to reconcile with them. The words of the General Catechetical Directory, "a form of the ministry of the word intended to make men's faiths alive and active through the light of instruction" offer one example. For the ideas of ministry and faith seem at odds both with the criteria of reasonableness and with that of independence of mind. So we have the odd situation of having to rely on accounts which treat religion as an objective phenomenon; those of unbelievers or those of believers prepared to discount for the time, the inner logic of their faith.

It is easy enough to see why this is. Those who wish to justify the place of religion in the curriculum will tend to set it on all fours with physics or social studies. They will tend to present it as a discipline, an area of experience or a realm of meaning open to investigation like any others. They will be reluctant to draw on private understandings which might be thought subjective or partisan or outside the forum of public check and control. This tendency is understandable and reasonable. Nevertheless, I do not think we should be too ready to abandon accounts of religion which come from inside the world of faith. I shall return to this point later.

I wish now to discuss three accounts of religion and its place in education. Each of them gives it a place in the curriculum which has a different rationale. Consequently, each proposes different aims. The first of the three is that offered by John Wilson in *Education in Religion and the Emotions*. According to this view, the defining characteristic of religion is its connection with the emotion of awe. We are in awe of large, powerful and mysterious things, like thunderstorms, volcanoes or the sea; and of the superhuman powers which rightly or wrongly we believe to underlie them. Awe leads characteristically to worship. Religion, according to this definition, can be identified wherever awe and worship exist; from the Greek worship of Poseidon and the animism of primitive tribes, to the more refined and rational object of orthodox Christianity.

Most Christians, and especially Catholics, will find this account inadequate and unsatisfactory for several reasons. It does, however, set in high relief a weakness very typical of traditional Catholic education and, to some extent, of traditional Catholic life. The weakness is the tendency to set up an entirely rational scheme as though the essence of religion were a systematic corpus of doctrines. Wilson's thesis rightly recalls us to the recognition of the important link between religious education and the education of the emotions. We have sometimes treated the emotions as though they were superficial feelings which floated to on the surface of life. They are really a much deeper and more important part of our human endowment. When Pascal spoke of "the heart having its reasons", he was not referring to anything sentimental or irrational. He meant a way of apprehending and responding to reality; a way certainly subjective and highly personal, but not necessarily out of touch with rational and objective facts. Wilson also sees emotion as related to cognition. Awe involves not just raw feeling but also certain facts and beliefs about its object. One of the chief aims of emotional education will be to develop an appropriateness between the feeling and its object; so that we are not irrationally afraid or unreasonably guilty; but are afraid only of what is really fearful, guilty about what is really wrong and in awe only of what is in the old sense of the word, "awful" — mysterium tremendum, numinosum et fascinans.

For the moment, I will offer only one criticism of Wilson's account and that a purely logical one. It is that the definition attempts to be too comprehensive in trying to include every possible instance of "religion", including Poseidon and nature worship. An adequate complex concept does not need to include every possible example. For there is loose usage. There are aberrations; there is also a mainstream of meaning. If this can be identified other uses of the term can be left outside. If religion (or anything else for that matter) is too broadly defined it ceases to mean very much and it becomes impossible to go about living it or teaching it clearly. This is the case (a logical not an ideological one) to be brought against the inclusion in the religious curriculum of what humanists call "non-religious stances", or of Marxism. It is not primarily that these things are subversive or are not worthwhile. It is rather that if we expand the frontiers of "religion" indefinitely, shortly we shall not know where we are.

This consideration brings me neatly to my second account of religion, for here the word is defined more pre-

40

cisely and more narrowly. I take as a "case" of this view, a popular book by Michael Grimmit called *"What can I do in R.E.?"* It is true that what Grimmit says about the essence of religion is rather thin. Rather than define it like Wilson in terms of the emotion of awe, he seems to take Tillich's concept of "ultimacy" as the root one. But he achieves greater precision by adopting the six dimensions of religion proposed by Professor Ninian Smart, as the ways in which the ultimate mystery is expressed. These dimensions are the mythological, the doctrinal, the ethical, the ritual, the expressential and the social. They constitute a much more adequate account of religion than the earlier one. Though it has to be said that not every religion manifests all these dimensions and that in some religions, one dimension seems to dominate. Still they do provide already a basis and aims for the religious curriculum.

It will set out to initiate children into all the discussions of religion in a rational way which provides independence of mind. Thus it will meet all the criteria of education, provided that, to safeguard the third one, no one religion is favoured but material is drawn impartially from a number of them. It is important to notice the difference between this idea and comparative religion. The latter is an objective study *of* religion. This approach sets out to be an education *in* religion. It tries to help the children to feel their way into different aspects of religious life, teacher and pupils joining for the moment in a willing suspension of disbelief. It is an important idea, already carefully formulated through the massive research and development of the Lancaster project; made popular and influential through Schools' Council Working Paper 36; rapidly becoming the new orthodoxy for religious education in County schools. In religious education in a church context, we have nothing that even comes near to matching it. Indeed very many of our difficulties in religious education stem precisely from the lack of a comprehensive and systematic theory such as this. I should like nonetheless, with respect and with some trepidation, to offer three reasons why I cannot accept the thesis which Michael Grimmit sets out.

My first quarrel with him concerns his distinction between confessional, non-confessional and phenomenological approaches. The first teaches one particular religious faith as true. The second favours one particular faith while acknowledging the value of others. The third shakes free entirely of commitment to any specific belief or content. It initiates generally into the world of religious life, drawing on whatever material is most appropriate. It is, Grimmit argues, "unbiassed" or "non-partisan" and it alone can count as education within the meaning of the Act. There are two points about this thesis which seem to me questionable. The first is the use of the category of the "neo-confessional" within which most of the religious education which goes on at present would probably fall. Grimmit includes in it what might be called broad-minded education — the gospel and the Church made relevant to the modern world. But he also includes the implicit religious approach; the view taken by Harold Loukes and also, I think, from very different premises by the view that religion is co-extensive with experience when that is appreciated in some depth. Now these are two very different things, and the way in which they are bundled together suggests to me that the three categories themselves are rather imprecise, and that the aims which they adopt need a more careful analysis.

The second objection I wish to raise concerns the logical reason why it is maintained that only the non-partisan, phenomenological approach can be accurately called education. The reason seems to be that the other two — confessional and non-confessional — infringe the second and third criteria, independence of mind. I do not see why this is logically necessary. Christianity, at least, with its long and strong tradition of theology and apologetics can hardly be denied the title of rational. Moreover, although much christian education may not, as a matter of empirical fact, have shown much respect for autonomy or independence of mind, this again does not seem to be a matter of logical necessity. For it is perfectly possible to conceive a style of christian education which would allow room for the development of critical thought within a community and a tradition of faith. Moreover, it is arguable that a decision against faith is only properly rational and responsible when it is made from the experience of a community faith, from having known it from inside, and this is a point I shall return to in my next section. My point here in brief is that the logical connection between the demands of education and non-confessionality, is a weak one. It would be perfectly possible logically to initiate children into the several dimensions of religious life in an educational way, while pre-supposing commitment to and choosing material from a particular religious tradition, Christianity, Judaism or Islam. The real reason I think for insisting on non-confessionality, is a rather vague desire to avoid indoctrination plus the particular difficulties of religious education in a society whose religious outlook is pluralist. To clarify and to meet those reasons would take me outside the scope of this argument.

My second objection to the Smart-Grimmit thesis, concerns the idea of a "willing suspension of disbelief". Both Wilson and Grimmit are at pains to argue that they are not recommending comparative religion and they are anxious to forestall the many objections to the introduction of that study in schools. They maintain that it is perfectly possible for a teacher who does not hold a particular faith to enter into the experience of it and to help his pupils to do the same. So they would deny the principle that only the insider can properly understand the game. Wilson puts the point piquantly. He said that you might as well argue that only a teacher who has lived in Stuart England could effectively teach the history of the period. However, I do not think the analogy holds. The reason is that there is in religion a quality of ultimacy which is not present in history or the arts. Religion entails a moral commitment which is not merely a consequence but is a part of the act of faith itself. St Paul's phrase "Doing truth" catches this point. So does Newman's remark that "the real safeguard of faith is a right state of heart". There is in religious understanding a complex interweaving of reason, emotion and moral commitment. It is for this reason that the insider, perhaps only the insider, sees most of the game. It is this fact which justifies, even educationally, religious education within a community of faith.

My third objection is that the religious dimensions in this thesis are placed on all fours with each other. Yet they are in any religious system, closely interrelated. Each has a different function, some have a predominance. In Christianity, I should like to underline the importance of the doctrinal dimension. It has no absolute primacy. But it does have a controlling function. Doctrine ensures the unity of the Church. It enables it to survive the variety of culture and of language. It ensures continuity and identity. Again in the field of emotion, as observed earlier, emotion has a "cognitive core". This is not to reduce emotion to cognition. It is to insist that emotion must have an appropriate target. In dealing with the religious emotions, this again emphasises the controlling function of reason and of doctrinal formulations. It seems to me that after ten years of eclipse it is time to look again at the question of the teaching of doctrine. It is a difficult problem, but it seems to me, very necessary to tackle it. There is some parallel here with the teaching and learning of language. For some years, the more systematic cognitive aspects of this — learning to spell for instance or learning grammar — have been submerged in a flood-tide of creative writing. The theory is that these abilities are learned incidentally. In practice this does not always happen. So, a new concern has grown up with finding new ways of teaching these abilities. No doubt what will emerge will be very different from old-style spelling and grammar lessons. But the function is the same. The necessity of learning these abilities explicitly is once more recognised. In a similar way, good doctrinal teaching will be very different from old-style parrot learning of doctrinal formulas. As the grammar lesson is based on a grammar of function, so doctrinal teaching will be based on the function of doctrine in the life of the Church and of the individual Christian. It will be enlightened by what we know now about the effective teaching and learning of cognitive material. Perhaps a properly systematic approach to it might provide a new impetus and a new interest in what will certainly be a difficult task. For, as Baron von Hugel observed, "Reasoning would appear to be the transferable part of the process but not to move us; and experience alone to have the moving power but not to be transferable". Doctrinal teaching will always be difficult from the point of view of interest and motivation. A new attempt at it would have to be carefully worked out and properly based on its relationship with other aspects of religious life. In suggesting that this should be done, I am not returning to the view that the substance of religious education is a body of doctrinal knowledge. I am arguing that doctrine is one indispensable and neglected part of religious education and religious life. Moreover, the learning of it is particularly appropriate to the school, a place concerned centrally though not exclusively with promoting knowledge and understanding.

Let me summarise at this point the phenomenological theory of religious education. It is a massive and impressive case; philosophised by Ninian Smart, made concrete and practical by Michael Grimmit, given an official benediction by Schools' Council Working Paper. We who are concerned with religious education in a church context, would be foolish to ignore it. We have nothing which even remotely matches it. Yet, as David took his slingshot to Goliath, even the isolated individual may find a weak spot in his forehead. I find three logical weak spots in it. *First*, the identification of "educational" with "non-confessional", is at least not proven. *Secondly*, the "empathetic" method which envisages the learning of religion by a temporary suspension of disbelief, may, in religious matters, not be possible. *Thirdly*, there is a case for saying that the "religious

45

dimensions" central to this approach, are not level-pegging with each other, but have different functions within a total scheme. If this is so, then the conclusions for the religious curriculum will be very different from those which Michael Grimmit draws in his book.

Finally, I wish to consider briefly an alternative and very different thesis put forward by W.D. Hudson in *New Essays in the Philosophy of Education*. Hudson also addresses himself first to the same question: What is religion? and consequently what is the basis of its place in the school curriculum? His reply is that the concept of religion and consequently the universe of discourse which we can accurately describe as religious has two defining characteristics. The first is that it accepts the concept of God which he defines as "transcendent consciousness and agency with which the believer as such has to do". The second is that it uses a particular style of language. To characterise this, Hudson adopts from J.L. Hudson the category of "performative" language; he means the kind of language which in some way brings about what it expresses. Examples are, the phrase "I will" in the marriage ceremony, or the phrase "I name this ship" in a launching ceremony. So religion has a conceptual content all of which is logically related to the idea of God. It also uses a style of language which expresses an active *relationship with God*, which like a sacrament, enacts what it signifies. These two aspects of religion Hudson describes as "theology" and "devotion". Taken in the sense in which he means them, they circumscribe religious discourse and religions. Religious education must work within these limits; given that the criteria of rationality and of autonomy are observed. Therefore, if you abandon the concept of God, or if you abandon this style of language, you are no longer engaging in religious education, though of course you may be engaging in education of some other kind.

This is plainly a narrower and more precise definition of religion, as well as a more traditional one. It would not leave much place for the study of Marxism or for comparative religion or even for the phenomenological approach which does leave room for non-religious stances. These matters of course might well be taken up in social or liberal or environmental studies and then might be related to the religious curriculum itself in various ways. It is a definition which has the virtue of not bending over backwards to include every possible case. It also throws light on some of the problems which I have raised earlier, especially on the questions concerned with "confessionality". For if this definition is right, then religious education not only can but must be in some sense confessional. It must confess God — its theological element; and it must confess him in an involved or committed way — its devotional element. Confessionality, it suggests, is not a black and white affair, it is a matter of degree. Any dealing with religion involves some limits. The dimensions of Smart and Grimmit set the limits very wide, they would allow most organised ideologies into the concepts. Wilson with his defining concept of awe sets the bounds wider still and wider. Hudson argues that the limits should be more narrowly prescribed. All are agreed that religious education must allow for the criteria of rationality and independence of mind. But where you draw the logical limits of religious discourse itself remains an open question.

I can now state, though very briefly and rather tentatively, my own position. There are elements in all the three theories which I have outlined which I think to be valid. From John Wilson I adopt the importance of the emotions in religious education and the idea of promoting an appropriateness between our feelings and their "targets". From Smart and Grimmit, I accept the six dimensions of religious life and readily adopt them as the basis of the religious curriculum. From Hudson I draw the lesson that the logic of religion demands that its limits are not drawn too broad lest in trying to include everything it ends up by meaning nothing.

I go on now, although extremely briefly and inadequately, to the second question, the question of taxonomy;

how to formulate from this body of theory, aims for religious education precise enough to be teased out into specific objectives and eventually into teaching material. I propose five principles from which these aims can be deduced. *First,* religious education should initiate children into all the dimensions of religious life. So, learning doctrine, studying scripture, experiencing liturgy and belonging to a religious community are all valid parts of the substance of religious education. *Secondly,* there is no logical requirement that these dimensions should be treated as though they were of equal value. So, a religious curriculum could reasonably allow to, say, the doctrinal dimension a controlling interest. *Thirdly,* educational criteria do not rule out that the teaching and learning might go on in a climate of commitment. Education can occur within a community of faith. But *fourthly,* the criteria of education do require that religion be rationally presented. Especially it is important that the curriculum distinguishes between belief and fact, and does not confuse religious and scientific certainties. And, *finally,* the teaching must be done in such a way that children's minds are not closed. It is this effort to shore up religious belief by irrational means against subsequent criticism. It is this rather than the nature of the material itself that really constitutes indoctrination.

There are two final questions. The first is to forestall an obvious objection to the case which I have been making out. It is the objection that what I have said is logically tidy but runs counter to practical experience. For to confine the religious curriculum rather more narrowly, to urge the teaching of explicitly religious material in however enlightened a way, will, it might be urged, put the children off. For in a secularised world, they do not take kindly to religious ideas or religious language. Better to attempt to deepen their grasp of secular experience and hope that religious understanding based on that will grow. I admit readily that I have been concerned mainly with logical considerations rather than with empirical facts, interest or motivation. It may be that these are so at odds with the logic of the case as to change the principles of the curriculum completely. On the other hand, logic has its own value in education. It may also be true that motivational difficulties stem not only from the pressures of a secularised world, but also from the vagueness and lack of inner coherence of the religious curriculum itself. A well-constructed curriculum generates its own dynamism. Its purposefulness is an inbuilt motivation. If we could offer that, perhaps it would be a very different story.

Finally, it may be said that to define narrowly the limits of the religious curriculum, is to narrow down the scope of the church school. This, I agree, is true. Schools cannot work miracles. There are some things in religious education which they can do well. Others lie beyond their scope. It is important at present to define as clearly as possible what, religiously speaking, the school can reasonably be expected to achieve. Beyond that, we must mobilise the other educational potential of our Church; which is very considerable. We must try to involve the whole of our church community in the task of religious education. It is as a contribution to this larger strategy that I hope that this consideration of the limits and possibilities of religion as a classroom subject may be of some value.

D

4

The Education of Conscience

"Thus conscience doth make cowards of us all". Hamlet's dilemma highlights one view of conscience which we may call the intense view; an extreme sensitivity to moral issues; an agonising conflict between moral alternatives which may cause a paralysis of action or even destroy man's sanity. It is significant that Hamlet was a man of the Renaissance, fresh from school at Wittenberg; newly emerged from the sturdy public morality of the Middle Ages; thrown back therefore on the inner moral resources of humanity itself. He was not unlike the image many people have of contemporary man, "come of age", taking hold of his own destiny and feeling the full force of moral decision and moral dilemma in his own person. In our own moral tradition, on the other hand, we often speak of "examining one's conscience" as though it were as simple and casual an affair as consulting one's watch or working through a checklist. Conscience is not a simple word. It is one spoken in many registers. It has a vast hinterland of meaning; a long and complex past; it focuses varied and often conflicting philosophies, theologies and physical traditions.

For us Christians at this time, conscience has become an important sector in the general crisis of our affairs. A strong case is made out for clean separation of morality and religion, and for a programme of secular moral education; whereas we have always been accustomed to teach

50

morality in a strong religious context if not to regard it as a sub-department of religion. Our society is, for better or worse, much more open and tolerant than even a few years ago. Young people find themselves legally and socially able to do pretty much as they choose; whereas we have relied a good deal on social sanctions, public opinion and the power of small groups to shore up our moral teaching, and we do not always find that our moral training stands up well to the demands of this new situation. Again a school of moralists proclaims, in the doctrine of situation ethics, that there are no moral acts which are in an absolute sense good or bad. Everything depends on situation and intention; whereas we have been used to a hard and fast code of christian behaviour. And church authority, usually so definite and so precise in moral matters, seems in the last decade to have become reluctant to pronounce on contemporary issues — unable even, some have said, to enforce its pronouncements. We recall the storm which greeted the publication of *Humanae Vitae* and the rather general terms in which the English hierarchy's directive on moral questions was couched.

Is it, as some maintain, that church authorities have become timid and over-sensitive, and the christian rank-and-file lax or rebellious? Or is it that man has really come of age and taken hold of his own destiny and that some radically new interpretation of christian morality is called for? In order to even sketch an answer to these questions we need to probe into the foundations of conscience, into the nature of moral judgements and moral life, and into the relationship between morality and religion. The material that faces us in trying to get to grips with these questions is very varied and complex. But it can be conveniently gathered round three conflicts; that between moral skills and moral values; that between autonomy and authority; and that between relationship and law. I shall elaborate each of these conflicts and then try to draw some conclusions about the right relationship between morality and religion and its educational implications.

51

Moral skills and moral values

One of the most prominent and most recurrent ideas in recent writing on moral education is the central one propounded by John Wilson in his *Introduction to Moral Education*. This is the notion that it might be possible to devise a programme based entirely on the skills or abilities which are necessary for moral behaviour, leaving aside any positive content of moral values. This view is peculiarly sympathetic to our times, to an open and pluralist society in which a variety of moral values is on offer and it is not possible to discern one set which is universally accepted. In such a society the old problem of how moral statements are to be justified becomes particularly acute; and it is hard to see how the uncritical transmission of any one set can avoid the charge of indoctrination.

For Wilson, intentional behaviour is the class to which moral action essentially belongs; that is the ability to act deliberately, for appropriate reasons, after reflection; not therefore from habit or from feeling or prejudice or in deference to public opinion. Of course, we often act for reasons which have nothing to do with morality. When we try to mark off those reasons which can validly count as moral, another range of problems arises. It becomes necessary to invoke, explicitly or implicitly, some definition of the nature of morality itself; and the ghost of all the controversies which have beset the history of ethics is raised again. Wilson offers as the defining characteristic of a moral reason that it is concerned with "other people's interests"; and this social or interpersonal ethic is certainly an important criterion, though not everyone would agree that it is an exhaustive one. Moreover intentional behaviour is not a purely intellectual affair. It involves emotional elements too and takes into account our dispositions and attitudes. Nevertheless, to place morality, in this way, is an important step forward. Perhaps it will be possible to precipitate out of morality a set of abilities which are not tied to any one religious or philosophical system but which are used by religious and secular moralities equally. The ability to foresee the consequences of one's actions, to construct a moral principle and apply it to concrete cases, to understand one's own feelings and to enter sympathetically into those of others: devise a programme to promote these and you will have a content-free system of moral education acceptable to all.

Perhaps this scheme gets us out of a nasty tangle a little too neatly to be wholly credible. I am not sure in the first place, whether, either in theory or in practice, the distinction between skills and values is as straightforward as Wilson claims. Is not, perhaps, this selection of skills that thought most important by the liberal West? And in practice, do not our values, our beliefs about life, enter into our moral living and moral education more positively and powerfully, so as deeply to affect the whole process? Then I wonder, at a more pragmatic level, whether the scheme is not rather utopian. The very sophisticated intellectual and emotional abilities involved are at present the possession of only a small élite. A substantial amount of research supports the view that abstract thinking and emotional discrimination both depend on early familiarity with a certain style of language common only in middle class families. The articulation of motive and intent and the envisaging of the consequences of one's actions are abilities seriously underdeveloped in people brought up solely on the restricted code. Maybe massive educational programmes and social changes will alter this situation. But it is doubtful whether, in the foreseeable future, these constituents of moral maturity will be sufficiently widespread to justify pinning to them our hopes for the whole moral future of our society.

In spite of these criticisms I believe that Wilson's theory does strike at one of the weakest points in our traditional Catholic moral education; that is its failure to develop the human abilities necessary for personal moral decisions; a failure which did not come to light in more stable times, but which becomes increasingly evident and serious as Christians in our complex world have to deal with new moral dilemmas with unpredictable situations or with new pressures. This failure has been partly due to the tendency, strong in recent Catholic moral teaching, to derive a comprehensive code of behaviour directly from religious premises, in the manner of *The Christian Rule of Life* and *The Christian's Daily Exercise*. This tendency to try to foresee every possible moral situation, and provide a ready-made answer, left little room for moral manoeuvre, and provided little training in the making of personal decisions or in any moral skill save that of uncritical obedience.

Another factor in traditional Catholic morality which has led to this weakness, is its very objective character. It has concerned itself mainly with the classification of acts. Mortal sin, venial sin, the commandments, the virtues — all of these have been worked out in terms of overt behaviour which fall within these categories. This approach has certainly the virtue of clarity, and many areas of behaviour may be correctly classified. Still, it draws attention away from the subjective factors crucial to the making of moral decisions; the attention to motive and reason, insight into one's own and others' feelings, sensitivity to situations and persons — the very skills of which Wilson speaks. We need to re-establish these subjective elements in moral theology, not as external factors, like excuses or mitigating circumstances, but at the very heart of that discipline. For moral theology should be more than the making of christian moral judgements, it should study the actual living of a christian moral life by persons in the flesh.

Autonomy and authority

A second word central to the discussion of moral education by psychologists, philosophers and theologians alike, is the word autonomy. The general meaning of the term is rational self-determination, but it will be worth looking at some of its shades of meaning, since it does contain several potential confusions. In Piaget's early account of the development of moral judgement, autonomy is the term of the developmental process. It means making up one's own mind about the rightness of actions, as opposed to accepting uncritically the rules which the adult world prescribes. It is marked by attention to the spirit of the law rather than its letter and is a judgement of motive and intention rather than of material constituents of the act.

Significantly and typically, Piaget labels this kind of moral outlook, co-operation. He believes that it arises solely from social interaction, that its only foundation is the demands of social life, and that the earlier morality of constraint is simply an infantile stage to be outgrown, and one which makes no positive contribution towards maturity. Authority in this scheme then has no positive part to play in moral development and at best must occupy itself in preserving order, while moral growth goes on independently. This is an important point because it means that constraint and authority in earlier childhood has a purely negative role in moral growth. The morality of constraint is something wholly to be outgrown. To control young children in this view, to form good habits and to impose rules on them, is something which in no way promotes moral growth and which should be abandoned as soon as possible.

This negative view of the role of authority has not been confirmed by later work following Piaget's lead. The American Kohlberg worked out a much more sophisticated developmental scheme of six stages. The fifth of these — a morality of contract and democratically accepted law — corresponded roughly with Piaget's autonomy. But Kohlberg found that in later adolescence another type of morality emerges characterised by the presence of individual principles of conscience. This does not depend wholly on accepting the demands of social life; these principles may derive from a new world-view, or from the rational and personal acceptance of traditional values. This finding is confirmed by the research of N.J. Bull who labels Piaget's final stage "socionomy" and uses the word autonomy to describe the stage in which personal values are accepted and lived by. An even more important deviation which Bull makes from Piaget's scheme is that he finds autonomy growing through the gradual internalising of precepts learned during the heteronomous stage. The possibility that the early morality of constraint might have a positive part to play in moral growth is an important one, to which I shall shortly return.

It is worth looking briefly at this point towards freudian theory. While Freud's superego, his unconscious conscience, and Piaget's heteronomous morality are clearly thought about in different registers, they have certain similarities. Both are forces in moral life which derive from adult prohibitions and controls on children's behaviour. It is significant that freudian theory, while emphasising the dangers of excessive superego development — the inhibited, guilt-ridden personality — does assign a positive role to the superego in personality growth. Defect may be as bad as excess. It is significant that the American social psychologists, Havighurst and Taba should confirm this. Their highest moral type, labelled "rational-altruistic", is a person whose superego development has been fairly strong, though not excessive — someone presumably therefore brought up with affection but with moderate strictness.

The word "autonomy" and the ideas associated with it are not unfamiliar in moral theology. St Augustine's words "Love and do what you will" is a classical statement of the fundamental independence of christian morality from external authority. Evil things, our Lord says in the gospel, come out from the heart of man and do not consist, at least in their essence, in the failure to observe external rules. And St Paul speaks very harshly of the power of law to distort men from the human true. Christians must be free of it, because they are children of God and must live by that, and not by external pressures.

It would be wrong, of course, to isolate this element in christian moral life from its context. St Augustine's advice presupposes rather than constitutes an unusually high degree of moral perfection; that of a person who has learned to love so truly and to know God so well that his desires are completely integrated by that love and there is no longer any moral conflict in him. Our Lord's words about the interior character of human good and evil, need to be complemented by his other words, "If you love me, keep my commandments" which clearly presuppose external laws and standards even if these are not very specific. Paul was inveighing against the excessive legalism of the jewish law which made it a crippling burden and obscured the presence of God's call and covenant which alone could give life to a code of behaviour. Moreover, in the history of christian morality, constantly, and from the beginning, a great deal of attention has been concentrated on laws, traditions and the solution of moral cases. The liberty of the Christian cannot be construed to mean that he is a moral vacuum, without moral guidance and directed only by charity. Nevertheless, at the heart of the gospel there is a reverence for personal freedom, for the inner autonomy of a decision made in the light of values as a necessary element in true human goodness.

This human value of personal freedom, together with its religious implication, is what the Second Vatican Council is acknowledging in its document on the autonomy of the individual conscience. When it has been lost sight of in an overgrowth of rules and conventions, we must try to recover it. And in christian moral education, autonomy understood in this way must be a constant criterion, indeed our compass-bearing.

Two concrete conclusions emerge from this discussion. First, in the upbringing of children, constraint, rules and the formation of good habits, discipline and control, have a positive part to play in moral growth. However, if discipline is too rigorous, if it is based on fear, or if it is persevered in too long, there will be a danger either of infantilism — that is the fixation of moral growth at a stage of blind conformity — or of total rejection. What seems to count is the way in which control is exercised. If adult authority appears — to Piaget for instance — as a negative force, I think this is because he wrongly reduces the relationship of adult and child to constraint alone — as though it were merely a series of prohibitions "Go and see what Johnny is doing and tell him not to". In fact it is part of a much larger relationship and its effect depends on the character of that relationship. If control is exercised in an atmosphere of affection and acceptance, maybe the precepts given will be the ones which, according to Bull, will become internalised and develop into personally accepted values. In her criticism of other parts of Piaget's work, Susan Isaacs speaks of his rather chilly developmental scheme as discounting "the emotional richness of the child's life". In his study of moral growth what is missing is the richness, variety and warmth which can and should characterise the child's relationship with a parent or with a teacher.

My second point is about the place of moral authority in adult life. Autonomy is a very adult concept indeed: "Love and do what you will" is advice for saints. Paul says the law is a tutor, it leads us to something which is better than law — the freedom of the children of God — but how many people can really outgrow it? This freedom is the highest of human achievements. It requires that we shake off not only the outer determinisms of force, habit and convention, but also the inner determinisms of illusion, fear, and concupiscence. And "Love and do what you will" requires also the final step of renouncing self-will and self-interest.

I do not think that the "autonomy" we may envisage as a realistic objective of moral education can be quite so lofty an ideal as that. Furthermore, the ideal is not only lofty but also perilous. For there is a fashionable pseudo-autonomy which masquerades as the real thing but turns out to be something very different. Conventional morality is sometimes decried as "bourgeois respectability" or as "Victorian taboos", and positive rejection of it is seen as the beginning of authentic moral life. Sometimes Christians may find themselves bound to reject conventional morality like the Berrigan brothers in America or like the Dean of Johannesburg. But this could not be done lightly. For to set up the autonomy of your own conscience against conventional morality is to run the risk of self-deception. It may be that you are right and heroic. But it must frequently be that you are the victim of wishful thinking. Conventional morality is wrong because you want it to be wrong. This pseudo-autonomy is not morality at all, but a life driven by whims and by self-interest.

Autonomy may well be a characteristic of moral life involving the acceptance of an existing code, even a strict one. A life can be rationally self-directive yet lean heavily on the traditional moral wisdom of the Church. The conditions would be first that there must be some process of interiorising or deepening through which these external rules become individual principles of conscience; not necessarily a dramatic identity crisis, but some process involving reasoning and criticism which would lead to a personal commitment; and secondly it is hard to conceive that such a moral outlook could be applied in a mechanical or legalistic way for such a process of interiorising would involve grasping for the spirit of the law and not stopping short at the letter.

Relationship and law

The third conflict has already cast its shadow before in some of my previous remarks. Traditional Catholic moral theology has been heavily naturalistic, relying on categories such as the nature of human acts, law, especially the natural law, essences and natures, deriving a great deal of its system from philosophical principles, especially from the aristotelian ethical system. Since this method in moral theology has recently come under heavy fire as being against the spirit of the gospel, it is worthwhile to begin by remarking its strengths.

John Macquarrie in his book *Three Issues in Ethics* notes two of these. The first is that this naturalistic approach to ethics offers more common ground with secular morality than does an exclusively evangelical ethic such as that adopted by Protestants of the school of Karl Barth. We need to see Catholic morality in a world context, related positively to the general moral striving of mankind. To achieve common ground we should work towards a shared anthropology, a common theory of man. Useful concepts such as natural law should not be dropped but re-interpreted in the light of contemporary man's understanding of his world. Secondly, while traditional Catholic morality often appears as a comprehensive and rigid code, in its method it is not that. Bernard Häring in an essay on the moral theology of St Alphonsus Liguori makes the point that this was essentially a casuistry, a series of cases offered to confessors as examples of how moral problems should be solved. It is not a compendium of the answers to all possible questions, but rather it works through the problem cases to show by what principles and by what processes concrete issues can be dealt with; not a calculus, therefore, but a series of case histories. Of course, such an approach easily becomes fossilised into a mechanical system or a rigid code. Still the method of casuistry has, I think, a lot to offer us in moral education.

Bernard Häring himself has led the reaction against the legalistic spirit in moral theology. In the first chapter of his great work, *The Law of Christ*, he insists that the essence of christian morality is to be not an ethic of law, not an ethic of essences and natures but an ethic of relationship. For the Christian, whatever categories may be used to work out his morality in the arena of public life and discourse, its inner reality, its very self, is the reality of his relationship with God and nothing else. It is dialogal; the word Häring uses to characterise it is the German word *verantwortung*, which means responsibility in a very personal sense, almost "responsiveness". To speak of morality in this way is to lift it out of the world of Wilson's moral skills or Piaget's rules of the game, or a set of social norms which are well or badly respected. We are speaking now in a different register. Morality appears now in a new depth, in a new perspective. It defines itself no longer in terms of regulated behaviour, the calculation of consequences or the observance of codes. It defines itself, now, in terms of the alienating force of sin, of the reconciling power of grace, of the mystery of christian hope, of the judgement of God's truth.

To speak of morality in this relational way, raises immediately the spectre of situation ethics. For the situationist also, a relationship — love — is the only true foundation of morality. Laws, essences and natures can be at most obliquely relevant. No overt action can be classified as always and everywhere wrong. What counts in any moral situation is only whether or not one acts in a loving way. Bishop Robinson in a well-known passage from *Honest to God* catches the spirit of this ethic well when he speaks of love as having "an inbuilt moral compass which enables it to 'home' intuitively on the needs of another".

Pure situationists, who are prepared to do without a moral code altogether and rely solely on the discerning power of a relationship, are few and far between. For the weaknesses of situation ethics as a moral theory are glaring; John Macquarrie in the book already referred to, sets out these weaknesses, succinctly and convincingly. Situation ethics disregards the similarities between human acts and considers only their uniqueness; and because of this, it fails to capitalise the moral experience of the race. By dividing moral life up into distinct situations, it destroys the unity of the personal self. It is incurably individualistic and incurably subjective. In its emphasis on the strength of love, it neglects the weaknesses of human nature. It offers no clear account of the extent and limits of a moral situation. The concept of love is in Bernard Häring's words "structureless". I have already referred to strengths of our traditional Catholic moral system, its clarity and exactness, its common and social character, its realistic awareness of human weakness, its quality of cumulative moral wisdom. It is true that it makes great use of the category of law or rule. But I do not think we should be too ready to abandon that category. In a well-known passage from *A Man for All Season*, Robert Bolt puts into the mouth of St Thomas More this defence of the law. St Thomas is arguing with his son-in-law Roper, who has been influenced by Reformation theology against what he regards as the over subtlety of Catholic thought. More remarks that the devil himself is entitled to the benefit of the law.

More: What would you do? Cut a great road through the law to get after the devil.

Roper: I'd cut down every law in England to do that.

More: Oh — and when the last law was down and the devil turned round on you, where would you hide Roper the laws being all flat? This country's planted thick with laws from coast to coast — Man's laws not God's — and if you cut them down — and you're just the man to do it — do you think you could stand upright in the wind that would blow then?

Roper: I have long suspected this; this is the golden calf, the law's your god.

More: Oh Roper. You're a fool. God's my God.

This argument is being rehearsed today wherever moral questions are discussed. The trouble with law (and probably with any other moral category) is not that it isn't useful. The trouble with it is that it is so useful that it has a way of taking over morality and occupying, there, the place that should belong to God alone.

Situation ethics is an influential movement. It is also a symptom of a deeper shift in our moral outlook, one which has affected christian as well as a secular morality.

I have already referred to Bernard Häring's definition of christian morality as "dialogal", essentially beginning with "responsiveness". We see the same shift of thought of work in religious education; the tendency here is to use the word "response" very widely, and to try to build a child's moral life on his relationship with others and with God, rather than initiating the child into a code of behaviour. The revolt against legalism, the movement to make christian morality both more human and more evangelical, certainly has its dangers. Nonetheless, it is the central tendency of christian moral thought at the present time.

Karl Rahner in an essay called "Situation Ethics in an Ecumenical Perspective" offers a sympathetic appraisal of this theory in relation to Catholic moral theology. It highlights those human and subjective elements — feelings, motive relationships, psychological and social pressures — which have made such a poor showing in our traditional textbooks. But the categories through which our moral system has been traditionally worked out — essences, natures and laws — are not excluded by this more personal approach to morality. On the contrary, these elements are a part of the situation in which we find ourselves and for the Christian they are part of that christian past which we can never disown but carry always on our backs.

There seems then to be two elements essential to an authentic christian morality, the element of relationship and the element of law and tradition. Without law, morality becomes anarchic, without relationship it becomes fossilised. The history of christian morality is a cyclic development around these two poles. It begins with a simple covenant of love, "You will be my people, and I will be your God". But immediately and necessarily, people ask, "How should this relationship be worked out in these situations which crop up in our daily lives?" In answer to this, a code of behaviour begins to be worked out which becomes eventually the crushing burden of the Pharisees. Then the New Covenant is proclaimed as a liberation. "The truth shall make you free". But **again** the converts are quickly asking, "What about meat offered to idols?" "Is it right to divorce a pagan wife?" And so the process of developing a comprehensive code of behaviour begins again. The problem for christian morality and moral education today is how to reconcile these two elements. Our moral education must root itself in the christian relationship to God and in essence must not be side-tracked into anything else. On the other hand, it must also offer realistic guidance to Christians trying to live out their faith in the contemporary world.

In conclusion I should like to say something first of all about religion and morality. The two are clearly not the same, nor can either of them annexe the other. The secular processes which govern behaviour — essences, natures, laws, principles, reason, feelings, relationships, moral situations, skills and cults — these are the same for all men. What religious faith does is to illuminate the whole moral process, so that its deepest meaning appears; to uncover the ultimate significance of human values; so that the Christian knows that his moral life is in fact the working out of his relationship with God. In this way, although the constituents of his moral life are the same as for anyone else, its totality is different.

Where does the moral authority of the Church fit into this picture? I remarked earlier that the idea of moral autonomy does not exclude moral authority, nor does the category of relationship obviate the necessity of some kind of code. What matters is that the authority be accepted through faith in what the Church is, and that the code be seen as the necessary structure of a religious relationship.

Now in a more stable and less literate society, a high degree of moral guidance was possible — even to an extent, necessary. The Church tried to envisage every possible moral situation and to provide a comprehensive moral code. Our society is no longer stable — it changes fast and constantly throws up new and disturbing moral issues. Moreover it is literate and sophisticated.

We know much more about ourselves, about the forces within us which influence us towards decisions. In this situation, as Karl Rahner observes, the Church can go less far down the road from general principles to concrete cases. Christians in the modern world must be trained in what he calls "the holy art of finding the concrete prescription for his own decision in the personal call of God, in other words the logic of concrete particular decision which of course does justice to eternal regulative principles".

It is this "holy art" which is the objective of christian moral education. It requires first of all, sensitivity to the call of God in our own lives, that is to say it is of a piece with education in faith. It cannot live unless as part of a living relationship. Yet it also requires the development of those intellectual and emotional abilities which constitute a moral decision. And while the contemporary Christian in a complex, pluralist, unstable society needs a fair measure of moral autonomy, he needs also to belong properly in that community of moral wisdom which is the Church, attentive to its past and to its living voice. Not everyone can be an expert in moral theology. But every Catholic, especially if he is a teacher, should know enough moral theology to be able to assess the weight which must be given to the different kinds of moral teaching which exists in the Church. It is not easy to do this. In dogmatic questions, theological notes are usually attached to propositions — of divine faith, of Catholic faith, common teaching and so on; and these are a useful shorthand way of assessing the depth in which the Church is committed to these propositions. There is at present no parallel way of estimating the degree to which the Church has committed herself in moral teaching which theologians would "consider to be an infallible statement". Still there is obviously a profound difference between a papal encyclical and the teaching of an individual bishop;

E

between the opinion of a school of theologians, and universal confessional practice over several generations. In presenting the Church's moral truth, we need to make these discriminations so that the central tendencies of christian morality appear, and so that we neither abandon what is permanently valid, nor absolutise what is ephemeral.

Our world, as the General Catechetical Directory observes, is "a world difficult to understand". Only seven years ago, I characterised it as "the world of 'O Calcutta' and the little red book, though also of Mother Teresa of Calcutta and Jesus Christ Superstar; the world of ecology and interplanetary travel, the world of LSD and organ-transplants, the world of student-power and black-power, of computer-technology and 'Kathy Come Home'". How dated that sounds already. The future is another country. They do things differently there. Yet the world of the future is as much God's country as the world of the past. And we have a different responsibility to it. The world of our grandparents is altogether out of our reach. But our grandchildren will have to face moral and religious problems which we cannot even imagine. There are things we can do to help them to cope with it.

In the first place christian moral education begins with education in faith. To believe is ultimately to see the world and its issues in a certain light, the light of God's call and man's response. While this may not solve many concrete problems, it provides a perspective without which christian morality cannot exist at all. For the moral world of the Christian does not stop short at the rational calculation of consequence. Its true geography is made up of the mysterious realities of sin and grace, of freedom and man's eternal destiny. Christian moral values are rooted in faith and it is worth remembering that the transmission of values probably depends more on the implicit quality of life of the school as a christian educative community than it does on the explicit word of the religious lesson.

Secondly, we need to strengthen our teaching of moral

skills for the Christian of the future will need to be much more morally autonomous than the Christian of the past. So rapid and so profound are the changes in our lives that the Church's moral teaching, depending as it does on study, reflection and experience, cannot possibly produce well-packaged answers to every moral problem quickly. Children must grow up able to stand morally on their own feet and to cope with their own dilemmas. We should remember that many subjects and many aspects of the school curriculum can have moral objectives; they can promote the abilities whether intellectual or emotional which are necessary to a human moral decision. We ought to try as curriculum theory develops in scope and influence, to formulate these objectives carefully, and plan programmes of work to realise them.

But thirdly as a counterweight to this, we also need to offer to all children, especially the younger ones, specific christian moral teaching. And here the keynote should be, as in all religious education, that central things should be central and marginal things marginal. We must emphasise those teachings behind which the Church has put the full weight of her moral authority. We must not over-emphasise, as we have in the past, certain areas of moral life in so negative a way as to surround them with irrational guilt. It will be necessary to teach a code to some extent. But in presenting the Church's teaching we ought to remember that our deeper aim is to bring children inside the community of moral wisdom which is guaranteed by God's word, but which is also living and therefore developing. It is as members of that community that they can learn the holy art of translating general principles into concrete decisions which is the central concern of the formation of conscience.

5

Some Questions
about Religion and Counselling

Although this paper is cast in the form of a series of
questions, it contains a tentative thesis; rather an untidy,
half-worked out one, but one which I think of some
importance to those whose work spans the two worlds
of counselling and religion.

In a paper called "Lieben und Arbeiten; a case of cake
and eat it", Liam Hudson puts forward the following
thesis. People are drawn into psychology, mainly because
of certain temperamental qualities, interests and values
that they have. In Freud's prescription they lean to lieben
rather than to arbeiten. Personal autonomy, creativity and
warmth in personal relations are the things they prize
most highly. Yet, Hudson argues, many people live creative
and socially useful lives even though their "lieben", their
personal world of loving, is an unholy mess. Psychologists
tend to misjudge, to underrate these lives.

"Psychologists, in other words, do their best to live
fully both intellectually and personally, but the evidence
suggests that they pull off this feat only occasionally. It
seems likely, therefore, that psychologists have used their
own goals in life — lieben und arbeiten — as a prescription
for Everyman. On this argument, anyone unlike a psycho-
logist is automatically judged limited or neurotic. I would
argue that, on the contrary, although there are many

different tactics and priorities which we use in coping with the pressures of our work and private lives, no one tactic is intrinsically worse or better than any other. Each has it own characteristic weaknesses and strengths; and the neurotic is not the man who adopts one particular intellectual and personal style, but the one who having adopted a style suffers its weaknesses without enjoying its strengths".

It seems to me possible that the world of counselling might suffer from a similar weakness. Perhaps counsellors are on the whole a particular kind of person. Perhaps they reflect in their work a certain idea of human perfection, an *arete* as Aristotle worded it, an idea of excellence. Maybe this is a valuable ideal but a limited one which is easily led into certain distortions.

I should like to explore this theme along four avenues. *First* I will say something about the key idea of relationship. This is a many-sided idea and one which flourishes in several different contexts; also a very central one to both counselling and religion. *Secondly* I would like to look at personal autonomy and non-directiveness, and at what I want to call the "adult thesis" about Christianity. *Thirdly* I would like to speak of what I wish to call the fluidity of modern thought about life. *Fourthly* I will try to face a fact which is a very awkward one to those concerned with counselling or therapy or pastoral care. This is the fact, however you understand it, of the newness of the christian life. Finally I should like to plead, where counselling goes on in a christian context, for a certain theological stiffening.

1. *"Relationship"*

I wouldn't care to offer any kind of definition of this word. I expect that it has some clear core of meaning; also I think a large and vague penumbra, like the rings round Saturn. Interpersonal relationships of an immediate and fairly vivid sort are clearly important to most people; though there is a small number — for instance hermits — who seem to be able to do without them. I doubt whether a life conceived totally in the absence of some idea of relationship could be said to be properly human.

There is a strong tendency to use the word relationship fairly centrally in interpreting and giving value to psychological and moral reality. This is true not only of many psychological writers but also of a moral theologian like Bernard Häring who writes: "the essence of christian morality is to be a morality not of rules and principles, not of essences and natures, but a morality of relationships". I take it what all these writers mean is that the expression of mutual feeling, the smoothness and fruitfulness of personal interaction, the ability to make and stand by choices in view of other people's interests constitute worth in human life, in a way that nothing else does. We cannot read the holy scriptures or participate in the liturgy for long without noticing the dominance of the word "covenant". This although it often suggests the meaning of a legal agreement has much more the sense of mutual compact of self-giving. A great deal of our theology as well as much of the ethics of the New Testament, centres around the word.

It is only fair, if we are to stress the strength and the value of the word "relationship" to say something also about its weakness. There is first of all the fact that it is an extremely slippery customer, not only very difficult to catch by the tail but also having a chameleon-like quality which makes it usable for almost any purpose and in almost any way. This somewhat wraithlike quality comes out clearly if we contrast the idea of relationship with the concept of law, another very popular and very influential category in moral and social thinking. Law, very clear, very practical, very Roman, has the opposite virtues and weaknesses to the idea of relationship.

I have discussed the connection between the two and

the difficult balance which must be kept between them in another of the essays in this book.[1]

The values implicit in the idea of relationship all chime in the same register. They are the values of maturity, cordiality, happiness, openness, inner peace. I think it is important to say that those values are not altogether beyond criticism. Plato, for example, would have thought very little of them. He would have thought them typical of man's lowest, most unregenerate state; man chained so as to view only a shadow of a shade, only reality at third remove: man not yet resolved to be a pilgrim of the absolute; man not yet even beginning to turn towards those essences, static, fixed and final, which alone are truly real, towards the form of the good. Many oriental sages would take a similar view. I do not think we can shrug off Plato's view as wholly mistaken. Catholic theology is full of essences and natures which are hard to grasp and even harder to live by. These no doubt have to be reinterpreted. But the nature of christian tradition is such that we cannot ever totally disown the past; though christian morality, like doctrine, develops.

In this connection we might notice also the writings of some psychologists — logotherapists and others — who wish to bring values — substance rather than process, the fixed rather than the fluid — into their dealings with psychological reality itself. So they speak of neurosis as a flight from meaning. And meaning I think, almost by definition, is a point of reference outside the process itself which gives it significance. Meaning might be the terminus of a process; or it might be an overarching purpose which gives substance to the whole. I think we might say of christian morality that it consists in relationships which have a strong injection of meaning. This

---

[1] See Chapter 4, "The Education of Conscience".

meaning we might argue not only explains the relationship more deeply. It may also alter its character and structure; as sacraments we believe not only express something that is already in us but also bring into being something that is new. I am not in this section arguing against the importance of the idea or the reality of relationship in human life. On the contrary, I think it holds pride of place. I am only saying that unless it is complemented by — or includes — some other ideas — essences, natures, values, principles, meanings — it is liable to degenerate into a general mess of imprecision of feeling.

2. *Personal Autonomy*

Many theories of counselling, like many approaches to moral education today, give a central place to the development of personal autonomy; the ability to make up your own mind on moral and personal issues. The methods which are used to achieve this are variously designated as non-directiveness or teacher-neutrality. They involve to a greater or lesser extent the idea that a counsellor or teacher should not allow his own values or beliefs to obtrude influentially. His methods should be directed to enabling or stimulating clients or pupils towards autonomous decisions about belief or behaviour. In religion the same idea occurs in the form that I have referred to elsewhere as "the adult thesis".[2]

I am sure that there is a great deal of truth in this thesis. Christians, especially today, must grow up. They do not live in a tight little folk-culture, but in diaspora country, in an environment which is sometimes hostile, more often apathetic or pre-occupied with other things. Their faith must not be one which rests on insecurity

---

[1] See Chapter 6, "Adult Education and the Theology of Childhood".

or on custom. It must stand upon, at least, grow towards a free and personal choice. Education and counselling both, rightly work for the development of inner strengths.

Yet these ideas must be set in the perspective of the gospel. A religion which centres on human strength must seem strange to Christians who take to heart its teachings about poverty and failure. What is religion anyway? Is it a kind of strength or a kind of weakness? Is it something in the mind, a set of concepts and ideas? Or something out there in the social order — institutions, rules, and systems? Perhaps it is all these things, or something else quite different which contains them all and resists reduction. Certainly if it is a kind of strength, it is also a kind of weakness, and if we lose hold of that second half our theology gets badly distorted. Christianity always goes astray when it becomes a religion of human self-perfection.

Personal autonomy in faith, morals and personal life is increasingly an important ideal. But in stressing it, counselling must make room both in theory and in practice for human weakness, theologically for original sin. When it is practised in a christian context, it must also find a place for the value which christian faith places on suffering and failure. It should not fall into the cult of success — and I do not here mean financial success particularly, but generally, success in the project of life. It should avoid being so dedicated to personal autonomy that it subjects the poor of Jahwe to gales they cannot possibly stand upright in.

3. The Fluidity of Modern Life

I should like to begin this section with a quotation from Iris Murdoch's novel, *The Nice and the Good*. One of the characters in this novel is Jessica, an art teacher, product of a modern art school. The novel describes the atmosphere — in every sense permissive — which formed her there and writes:

Perpetual change and no hard feelings was the general rule and one which had kept Jessica, who religiously obeyed it, both inexperienced and in a sense uncorrupted and innocent. There was a kind of honesty in her mode of life. Her integrity took the form of a contempt for the fixed, the permanent, the solid, in general "the old", a contempt which, as she grew older herself, became a sort of deep fear. So it was that some poor untutored craving in her for the Absolute, for that which after all is most fixed, most solid and most old, had to express itself incognito. So Jessica sought to create and love that which was perfect but momentary.

This was the zeal, this the fanaticism, which she attempted to communicate to the children whom she taught at school. She taught them to work with paper, which could be crumpled up at the end of the lesson, with plasticine, which could be squeezed back into shapeless lumps, with bricks and stones and coloured balls which could be jumbled together again; and if paint was spread upon a white surface it was to move like a river, like a mist, like the changing formations of the world of clouds. No one was ever allowed to copy anything; and a little boy who once wanted to take one of his paper constructions home to show his mother was severely reprimanded. "So it's all play, Miss?" a child had said to Jessica at last in a puzzled tone. At that moment Jessica felt the glowing pride of the successful teacher.

In the novel, Kate, the central character, is the exponent of niceness. She runs a large, expansive household — family, friends, lame dogs — and her object is to "keep her people comfortable". Everybody in the community must be looked after, the social wheels must all turn smoothly. The eruption into her cosy little world of both goodness and evil of a much more vivid and powerful kind, brings the value of the whole enterprise into question. The characters find themselves confronted by painful ethical dilemmas by present catastrophes, by the resurrection of tragedies from the past. Quickly the moral landscape of the novel changes. Suddenly the identification of the nice and the good is challenged, the well-ordered, warm-hearted kind little community seems to be overturned by the emergence of a dominant, if rather strident major theme. A morality which is fluid, mobile, smooth, well-oiled is faced with a morality with much sharper edges, one which is indeed, a little grim.

At the end of Henry James' story *The Golden Bown*, a similar note is struck. The prince, a Renaissance charmer, certainly nice, though not particularly good, is having an affair with his former mistress. His wife's behaviour strikes a note of moral heroism, a kind of goodness quite foreign to his own moral landscape, and he is able to recognise and respond to it.

The idea that life, reality, is essentially fluid is not a new one. Many centuries ago the early Greek philosophers first began to ask the question: What is real? What is the essence of things? One of them — Heraclitus — answered that it was none of the elements that you would expect — not fire, not air, not water, but change itself. But the idea that fluidity, flexibility and change represent the dominant in life does exist today with a new and pervasive force. This is one reason, I think, why the idea of relationship is so popular. It also has about it something of the tentative, fluid quality which fits in with the climate of the times. Similarly, I think that situation ethics is popular not only because it represents a tenable ethical theory, but also because it appeals to those who are impressed above all by the variety, the kaleidoscopic quality of life today:

"Life like a dome of many-coloured glass
  Stains the white radiance of eternity".

The fluidity of modern life poses many problems for the Christian. What is permanent? What lasts? What is impervious to the probes of history and hermeneutics? In morality how much attention should we give to objective external acts? How far are they dissolved into the cloud-world of circumstance and situation? What validity has the traditional morality of "your station and your duties" against the idea of the lonely individual, finding his way across a constantly changing moral landscape?

Has Christianity an anthropology, a permanent "theory of man"? Is this something given and unchangeable, a fixed essence? Or is there room for the idea of man as "project", shaping his own future? In the development of faith and the life and teaching of our Church, we are just as vulnerable as anyone to the climate of fluidity. We do well to be ready for change and not to be afraid of it. Nevertheless, it is not good to be the victim of a force which may after all be nothing more than a fashion, the swing of a pendulum. Newman ended his *Essay on the Development of Doctrine*:

> "In a higher world it is otherwise, but here below to live is to change and to be perfect is to have changed often".

Yet the real substance of that famous essay is not so much change as identity; his question was: How can an idea adapt to the many vicissitudes of history and yet remain essentially the same? Rootedness — and this means being possessed by our faith in its historical development, its "unrolling" as Baron von Hugel said, — is essential if we are to change without evaporating.

4. *The newness of the christian life*

"You are", St Paul says, "a new creation". This newness has been variously interpreted, sometimes maximised, sometimes minimised. As a member of the Body of Christ, you have a new reality in you, the reality of grace. Connected with this — following upon it — is a new code of moral and spiritual practice.

In this reading, morals and principles and rules — for instance in sexual morality — are often deduced directly from a "given" revelation without the intervention of much understanding of how human nature works as the human sciences reveal that: though it is worth noting that it is frequently mediated through a classical, Greek philosophy.

The charismatic movement understands the matter differently. For its members this newness, this presence of grace is the Spirit's power inwardly experienced, re-shaping and transforming the felt inner self. It is that presence which is the principle of new life and a new source of action.

How strongly should this idea of "newness" or "differentness" be pitched? Should we minimise it by assimilating as much as possible of what the human sciences tell us into morality, into personal and spiritual life? Or should it strike a strong note through which our interpretations and our pastoral actions are drastically altered? Is it religion as dull habit or religion as acute fever?

The work of christian organisations concerned with counselling highlights this question sharply. Their very title presupposes differentness, distinctiveness, but in what should this distinctiveness consist? Should it be merely a "service" offered to others not differing except in motivation from that given by any secular agency? Or ought there to be some major difference in substance, in the way in which the task is done and the principles on which it works?

At the moment there is a tendency to minimise this distinctiveness; to reduce it to realities or processes derived from the human sciences, from group dynamics or from psychotherapy. So the Sacraments effect reconciliation into a supportive community of openness and warmth in personal relationships or balance and synthesis in the inner self. It is true of course that there has always been a tendency to interpret the gospel in terms of categories which seemed available and suitable — usually philosophical ones. It is a question how far this process can be carried forward before a fresh, distinctive, sometimes discordant note deriving from the gospel and the world of faith is — sometimes disturbingly — struck.

Sometimes the doctrine of the incarnation is invoked in favour of this reductionist view. Sometimes it is invoked simply as a way of canonising the existing state of affairs; of surrounding with a faint aura of divinity the dynamics of human living. As Newman showed in *The Arians of the Fourth Century*, this account is too superficial to stand up for long. The Nestorians (who, as Fr Congar pointed out, represent the dominant tendency of the last century or so) absorb the humanity of Christ in his divinity. So everything to do with religion becomes divine, beyond question, detached from human affairs. The Arians on the other hand, absorb his divinity in his humanity so that everything humanly worthwhile can be simply canonised. As Newman pointed out, Athanasius and Catholic orthodoxy see the danger of each of these views — not only as a doctrinal concept but as a way of viewing the world.

Equally we might look at the question from the eternally unresolved, yet perennially important point of view of the controversy about nature and grace. Is there a sharp frontier between the two? It is easy to say, "grace builds on nature", harder to detect the presence or action of grace in the world — in religious education or sexuality or work. I believe that Rahner's idea of the "supernatural existential" might offer a theological basis for pastoral initiatives in all these fields. Man's consciousness and his ideals form a horizon which is potentially limitless. These unbounded hopes, this quest for life and truth, meet the gift of life and truth which comes from beyond ourselves. This gift may well change, even radically, the quality, even the substance of our life and work. But it demands of us a kind of receptivity, a true sense of our own inadequacy. This opens the way to the gift of grace and enables it to work in us. It does not destroy initiative or enterprise. It does require a denial of our own self-sufficiency — the virtue which spiritual writers speak of as humility and to which they attach, rightly, such importance.

Counselling is an activity particularly vulnerable to fashion and change, particularly likely, as St Paul said, to be "blown about by every wind of doctrine". It seems to me particularly important that Christians who engage in it should possess a very firm basis for a critique of its changing fashions — a critique, not a rejection. This critical foundation I believe to be dependent on a certain theological stiffening. I do not mean by this that I think theologians, or even church leaders, should run everything. I think that a theologian's role in counselling, should be rather like that of an engineer in the building of a bridge. He should bring his own special insights to bear on it, while being aware of and sensitive to, the special abilities of others — of philosophers, psychotherapists and sociologists.

A particularly vivid example of this is the theological idea of "sacramentality" — a theological principle we might say, rather than a specific concept. Recent pastoral-liturgical renewal has touched the matter of sickness and death ("The Anointing and Pastoral Care of the Sick") of how you become a Christian ("The Christian Initiation of Adults") and of sinfulness and failure ("The Renewed Rite of Penance"). In each of these cases the renewal has taken the form of seeing a sacrament as the central point of a whole area of human experience and pastoral concern.

I wonder why it is that we do not have, even in prospect a renewed rite centred on the pastoral care of the married. Renewed rites are not only a way of canonising the status quo. They assert, effect and direct the new christian meaning of an area of life. They bring a new force into it. The presence of a distinctive and a forceful newness in counselling — whether in marriage or in any other area, is the urgent need which I wish, not dogmatically but deliberately, to put forward.

6

Adult Education
and the Theology of Childhood

In the most famous of Bede's *Stories*, a pagan priest compared the life of man with the flight of a sparrow through a banqueting hall. "It enters in at one door and quickly flies out through the other. For a few moments it is inside, the storm and wintry tempest cannot touch it, but after the briefest moment of calm, it flies from your sight, out of the wintry storm and into it again. So this life of man appears but for a moment, what follows or indeed what went before, we know not at all". This image of human life — confused, dazzled and vulnerable in its moment of light — seems so "naturaliter christiana" that it is no wonder Paulinus had little difficulty in converting the whole assembly. The human condition is to be helpless and lost, in need of understanding and redemption from beyond. Here is Paulinus with the word which enlightens and the grace which transforms.

Very likely at some time or other, all human beings feel that existential dread, that lostness and strangeness of their condition. But in modern times, men are much more at home in their environment. Such flashes of metaphysical puzzlement seem like fleeting fits of distraction from the real business of living. Man has come of age. No longer at the mercy of nature, he controls his destiny and can shape his future as he chooses. It is a different

81

image of life; that of a masterful intelligence, foreseeing, planning, controlling; no longer the victims of events but the maker of history.

Though Bede would never have formulated it this way, the image of the human condition implicit in his story is the image of the child, vulnerable, insecurely lodged in his world. The image in our talk about ourselves, is that of the adult, reflective, free, in charge of his destiny.

A dominant idea in our thought and talk about mankind is influential in many ways. I am concerned in this essay with its effects on theology and on education. The moral theologian, for example, is much less concerned to establish a moral order of essences and natures to which men must submit themselves. His interest is much more in the process through which a Christian who is a free and thoughtful human being, comes to make a personal moral decision. In education, also, the reflective critical person has become an educational ideal. He is initiated, no doubt, into ways of thinking and feeling which we inherit from the past. But he must learn to be autonomous within them, to stand on his own feet and to strike out his own line. Educators nod respectfully to the worthwhileness of the experiences of childhood and pass on. The "business of being seven" had to be got through. But its purpose is to make a success of being eight. The emphasis is on promoting the growth of those abilities which are thought best for the modern adult. To be critical, to be logical, to think empirically, to possess emotional discrimination; there, many people think, is where human excellence is to be found. Many regard childhood and what it stands for as a stage to be got through, whose purpose is merely to provide a foundation for what really counts in life. Once lived through it can be shed, only a shell or husk of meaning which must wear out before the kernel of reality can appear.

It is surprising that Christians are not more critical of this idea. It is true that we also believe life to be a pilgrimage in search of our true selves. But we cannot think of any phase of it as mere scaffolding within which the real thing is being built. On the contrary, at every stage of our lives we stand before God's judgement and in his grace. What counts in the end — though in an evolutionary pattern — is the content of our lives as a whole. No time, no stage, no season is lost irrevocably in the past. Each has, alongside its inescapable and tragic transience, an equally inescapable and sometimes tragic permanence. We cannot accept uncritically an idea of adulthood which discards childhood as mere preparation. Nor should we use the words "childish" or "infantile" as easy dismissive adjectives as though the judgements involved were simple black-and-white ones. Yet it is easy to see how adult faith has come to seem so important an ideal. Christians no longer live in a safe little subculture. They are scattered, in "diaspora". The climate of their lives is a variety of beliefs and moralities. The mass media bring this vividly home to them from their early years. In church life as well as in the secular world, they have to live with frequent change. New and complex situations demand difficult personal decisions. It is clear that the faith which will thrive best in this world is one which can stand on its own feet, is thoughtful, well-informed, rooted in personal commitment; an adult faith.

Out of these considerations has grown the adult thesis about Christianity. In the first part of this essay, I wish to offer a critical but positive account of it. In the second part, I will try to discern the values and realities of childhood which are of permanent worth; which even a religious life and education which bases itself on the idea of adulthood must take seriously into account.

1 Adult Faith and Adult Education

The adult thesis begins from the principle that Christianity is essentially an adult religion. The free adherence to God in faith, that begins it, is an act only possible to

83

adults. A Christian should choose freely to cleave to God. His life should be a reflective, deliberate application of the teachings of the gospel to the situation of his own life. So his grasp of the faith should be deep and hence flexible enough to be applied to many and various concrete cases. He must have a fair insight into himself and a good understanding of the world around him. The adult Christian, in this sense, is a rather autonomous person; not someone other-directed who takes his colouring from the community he belongs to or from his own subconscious past. His religion is rooted in light and freedom, in deliberate decisions and mature relationships. Calm of mien and clear of eye, liberated from childhood hang-ups, guilt feelings and superstitious habits he walks his pilgrim way along the path of enlightenment. He has taken up his position, he stands on his own feet safe from all disquiet. He is able to interpret the changing landscape of life in the light of the principles of the gospel.

Needless to say, there are some fairly fundamental objections to this thesis. If I have caricatured it a bit it has been to give these objections force. The first of them is that if the true Christian really is like this, intelligent, reflective, emotionally balanced, personally fulfilled, there are not going to be many of him. For few achieve that kind of perfection. And those who do, are usually products of a certain type of background and a certain type of education. But a much more fundamental objection is raised by the words of Kirkegaard: "Christianity is a religion for slaves; and only slaves belong to it; and those who are slaves cannot help belonging to it". A bit dramatic maybe. Nevertheless it is true that Christianity is a religion for poor people. The "poor of Jahwe" are not only those without prosperity or property. They are those without security or peace of mind; they are the confused, the mentally handicapped, the families at risk, the uprooted and the anxious. Those thus without inner wealth will join the economically poor in having the best place in the kingdom. The first beatitude is not "Blessed are the rich in spirit". Christianity always goes astray when it becomes a religion of human self-perfection.

I raise these objections rather forcefully because they are objections to a position which contains a great deal of truth and of practical wisdom. It is all the more important that such a christian idea should not come adrift. However much we develop communities to support each other, increasingly the Christian is going to need a great deal of inner strength. For the forces he has to cope with are not external powers as in a time of persecution. They are forces which besiege the inner self. Perhaps if we look more closely at the ideas of adulthood in terms of inner strength, we shall find it is not so sophisticated nor so utopian as my caricature suggested. "Inner strength" is quite a popular word in psychology. It is used often by E.H. Erikson. He calls the final achievement of the mature human being "ego-integrity". It comes at the end of a long road along which seven other major conflicts have been negotiated, with some success, and a person has achieved trust, autonomy, initiative, industry, identity, intimacy and generativity, against the dark, sterile forces which threaten him. The final conflict is with despair in the face of the human condition and of death; as Christian had to defeat the Giant Despair in Doubting Castle before reaching the end of his pilgrimage. In this quality of ego-integrity, all the cumulative inner resources garnered from his past achievements are massed; a sense of meaning in oneself, and of order in the world, a sense of spiritual values.

In trying to describe this elusive quality of maturity or adulthood — a description which must always be rather arbitrary — the author I have found most helpful is Gordon Allport. I should like to say something about the three qualities he picks out — a generalisation of his studies in human development — as most characteristic of maturity.

The *first* of these is self-extension. It is the ability to put your energies, even your life, at the disposal of some cause, some value which is larger than you and which does not serve your self-interest. A little child who plays a game of cricket, throws down his bat when he's out and wanders off to do something different. He is using the game and it no longer ministers to his needs. An adult is able to give himself to the game of cricket or the game of life, or to politics or religion, the arts, science or the love and service of others. He is over the deep fear, the fear of belonging "to another or to others or to God".

The *second* quality is the ability to be objective about ourselves. The little child's frame of reference is his inner feelings. Things and people are judged in the light of that. The adult should be able to shift the frame of reference. He should be able to see our little life as part of a larger drama and to judge himself, people and events in the light of that. So his judgements are marked by reality and truthfulness. This ability to be objective about ourselves is closely linked to a sense of humour. For humour, too, involves shifting the frame of reference so that things appear in a different perspective.

The *third* quality of the mature person is that he has achieved a fair synthesis of himself, a personal inner unity. So there is no major dislocation between thoughts and feelings or between work and personal life or between moral ideals and practice. The ideas and feelings, the forces, needs and aspirations within us, are held together and shaped by some meaningful framework of beliefs. One recent school of thought in psychology, the logotherapists, emphasise the importance of this factor. For them, neurosis originates not so much in unconscious conflict as in the flight from meaning. Meaningfulness in our own life, meaningfulness in the world, is what holds the self together. And meaningfulness derives from beliefs and values.

It is not hard to see how these three factors in human maturity apply also in religious life. Self-extension because a good Christian must be able to devote himself to others, to work, and causes which bring him no immediate satisfaction. He must have that is, the virtues of charity and justice. In the work of renewing the Church, many of us find ourselves involved in arduous and long drawn-out committee work and administration. Nothing could be more soul-destroying. Yet it is a mark of adulthood to be prepared to shoulder those burdens and get on with them. There are two types of religion. One is basically infantile. It conceives of my God bestowing security and special favours on me and on my group. It is a religion which ministers to the self and it often crops up in very subtle forms. The other has a vision of God's universal creative and redemptive love, and subordinates personal life to that. It is in this that christian maturity is to be found.

Secondly, objectivity, the ability to see ourselves and our concerns in perspective, is really the essence of the virtue of humility, which is precisely the ability to be truthful and objective about ourselves; not to let our judgements be coloured by self-interest. There is also a collective humility. The Church strives to be like Christ; to empty herself of human grandeur and devote herself to the service and the redemption of mankind. Objectiveness enables us to accept our frequent human failures, both individually and collectively, as Christ accepted his.

Finally, the synthesis, the making-whole of life. It is here that education in the broad sense is most relevant. For this wholeness depends upon our beliefs, for us Christians on our faith. It is this which gives to experience the sharp edges of meaning which make plain its true outlines, make it liveable and productive.

It is not a question simply of holding the faith. It must bite on life and cut it to its true shape. It is no good having profound insights into the paschal mystery unless they cast some light on what happens next Monday morning, or how we cope with depression, or what we make of this difficult relationship, of that moral dilemma; or how we understand the life of this one dying of cancer, of that one whose marriage has collapsed. Besides being in this way relevant, the faith must also be *coherent*. A jumble of disparate doctrinal statements, moral rules and liturgical practices could never make anything meaningful. In presenting the faith, in learning and re-learning it, these two characteristics, inner coherence and relevance to experience, will contribute most to this aspect of christian maturity.

When we consider these elements in a concept of the adult Christian, they do not seem particularly sophisticated or intellectual though they are undoubtedly fairly rare. They appeared outstandingly in the life of Franz Jaggenstater, a simple German peasant of very little education; one of the very few who objected, after thought and on principle, to serving in Hitler's army and who persevered in this conviction till death.

These I think are the principles on which christian adult education should be based. When all the qualifications have been made and all the dangerous false trails viewed, it remains probably the most important development in religious education today. Plainly no single programme is going to emerge from these principles. The movement must advance along several fronts. At the moment, variety and experimentation should characterise it. Let us avoid utopian blueprints and go ahead with courageous and imaginative ventures.

2 Towards a Theology of Childhood

For many centuries the idea of the child was that he was a "little man". He was smaller than an adult in size and in attainments, smaller rather than different. In the Middle Ages he was even drawn like that. Childhood was a cut-down version of adult life, its norms, the norms of adulthood. In the child everything was in potency, nothing actually realised. The business of education was to bring into being what was not yet there; to enlarge what was there only in germ. The qualities of adult life were the source of its purposes and values. "That which every gentleman desires for his son" wrote Locke, "is contained I suppose, in these four things . . . virtue, wisdom, breeding and learning".

Religious education shared this outlook. The "Catechism of Christian Doctrine" which was its main substance, was a reach-me-down version of the treatises in text-books of theology. The moral and devotional life of the child too, was, for the most part, derived from adult morality and adult worship. He was to compose himself for sleep with his mind fixed on the four last things. He might confess the sin of "being discontented with his state in life". He might even learn the prayer, "Let blind and infatuated worldlings intoxicate themselves with the false joys of this world, I on the other hand . . .".

A quite different view of the child was heralded by Rousseau's *Emile*. He is said to have "invented the adolescent at the same time that James Watt invented the steam-engine". He invented the child too. His idea was that childhood has distinctive ways of thinking and feeling which have their own quality and value; quite independently of its relation to adult life. When he wrote "leave childhood to ripen in your children", he meant that human development should proceed at its own pace. In the image of "childhood ripening" he was also pointing to its own intrinsic worth.

Rousseau's vision was part of a larger movement. It was part of a reaction against an artificial, sophisticated and corrupt social order, against a late eighteenth century which seemed spent and jaded. Hence the re-kindling of interest in what seemed by contrast primitive and spontaneous — a return to older roots. Hence the Gothic revival, the renewed interest in Celtic antiquities, the cult of the noble savage. Some of these movements were themselves self-conscious and artificial — the construction of ha-ha's and castellated ruins, the "Gothick" novels. Yet in a really major writer like William Blake we also find the assertion of the value of childhood, not measured by but set over-against the adult social order. In his case the reaction was not so much against the mannered decadence of the eighteenth century correctness but rather against the ugly brutality of the Industrial Revolution. His vision of the charity children at St Paul's Cathedral may sound like a piece of sentimentalism

> "Oh what a multitude they seemed those flowers of
>   London town
> Seated in companies they sit with radiance all their
>   own.
> The hum of multitudes was there but multitudes
>   of lambs.
> Thousands of little boys and girls raising their
>   innocent hands".

against the corrosive power of the dark Satanic mills.

> "But most through midnight streets I hear
> How the youthful harlot's curse
> Blasts the new-born infant's tear
> And blights with plage the marriage hearse".

His vision was that childhood asserts a set of values — innocence, spontaneity, creativity, simplicity, against the vices of the adult social order — experience, convention, hypocrisy, cynicism.

This contrast largely explains the fascination which the theme of childhood had for nineteenth century writers. For the artist felt himself, like the child, to be an alien both from the tired correctness of eighteenth century society and also from the brutal materialism of industry; alien from it, yet crushed by it. So Keats wrote in his last years that the only fragments he could shore against his ruins were "the holiness of the heart's affections and the truth of the imagination".

Many writers in the nineteenth century took up in one way or another, the theme of childhood. In more recent times, Holden Caulfield in *The Catcher in the Rye* is a successor to Blake's charity children. Not an innocent child but an awkward adolescent, he travels, a picaresque anti-hero, through the adult world and finds all aspects of it "phoney". Many drop-out movements among young people represent a protest in favour of simplicity and directness, against a society which seems complex, artificial and constricting.

It seems a healthy protest. Yet it has led to some odd excesses. We find these in the novels of Dickens who did not, on the whole, handle the theme of childhood well. His "Little Nells" and "Little Dombeys" were the prototypes of innumerable angel-children in Victorian literature. They represented a retreat into sentimentalism; childhood was simply an escape into an imagined golden age of innocence, from the responsibilities and complexities of adult life. Significantly, few of them survived into adulthood, most being carried off early by mysterious and lingering diseases. They ended with Barrie's neurotic fixation in Peter Pan and Mary Rose; childhood as a refusal of maturity, ultimately a rejection of reality altogether.

A true and healthy approach to the theme of childhood does depend on an appreciation of the quality of childhood experience and its value in itself. It also avoids the trap of getting fixated there, acknowledging the necessity of socialisation and the demands of maturity. Wordsworth in *The Prelude* seems to hold this balance best. His sensitive presentation of the experiences of childhood embodies their permanent worth. Yet they are also developmental — ingredients of his mature "moral being".

> "Dust as we are, the immortal spirit grows
> Like harmony in music; there is a dark
> Inscrutable workmanship that reconciles
> Discordant elements, makes them cling together
> In one society. How strange that all
> The terrors pains and early miseries
> Regrets, vexations, lassitudes interfused
> Within my mind should e'er have borne a part
> And that a needful part in making up
> The calm existence that is mine when I
> Am worthy of myself".

Wordsworth's developmental view of childhood is in sharp contrast with that of a more technical expert, Jean Piaget. Piaget's view is that the early stages of life should simply be outgrown, shed like husks; that on the whole they have no permanent value, only a preparatory one. He often describes them as "autistic" (a word we associate with mental illness) or "egocentric" (usually a term of moral condemnation). It is true that the experiences of childhood contain primitive elements which have to be outgrown. It is true that they have a preparatory function. You cannot really be eight until you have got through the essential business of being seven. But this should not exclude their permanent value, their importance as ingredients of the moral being, the "best self" of adult life.

The wholly preparatory view of childhood has its counterpart in catechetical theory. It is the view that early religious life is a husk to be shed; ultimately that the child is pre-religious, except in some mysterious sense, hidden in the mercy of God. D.H. Lawrence wrote of the "tubby infant . . . who is only . . . a new little clue to a human being laid, soft and vulnerable on the face of the earth". Some believe that the baptised tubby infant is no more than a new little clue to a Christian. This view seems to me to be dangerously wrong.

The Church's practice of infant baptism asserts something about the child. The infant it teaches, is already a member of the Church, already shares in the new life of grace. It is possible to interpret that teaching in a restricted minimal way. The life of grace, this argument would run, exists secretly beyond perception. What is observable and conscious about christian life exists not in the child himself but in his family and in the church community. They enfold the child in their corporate faith. If we want to see what the religion of childhood is, it is there that we must look.

There is a good deal of truth in this view. It is entirely true of the tiny baby. But tubby infants are not tiny babies. They have already made great strides in human development. Must we not say that their religious life has developed too? Of course, the religious life of young children is restricted in many ways. Their cognitive limitations mean that their understanding of the faith must be rudimentary. Moreover their ability to make free choices is slight. Nevertheless there are religious experiences in childhood which are of permanent worth. They constitute the child as a conscious Christian rather than, so to speak, a vicarious one. They are moreover experiences which a mature and adult faith requires if it is to be properly rooted.

First of all I believe (though it would be hard to prove) that children have a native sense of wonder. It is really the awareness that things are which precedes the investigation and analysis of what they are. This Wordsworth also believed even if he tied it, rather fancifully, to a theory of pre-existence. It does depend upon the awareness of existence rather than essence. "True learning" wrote William Walsh, "begins in wonder, goes on in humility and ends in gratitude". He believed that the sense of wonder which begins in childhood, should persist even into the most sophisticated adult activity, that of scholarship; if, that is, scholarship is to be more than mere conceptual cleverness, the adroit manipulation of ideas, the separation of variables. A sense of wonder should also persist in good theology, which is why quite small children occasionally ask extremely difficult theological questions. Good theology should not stop short at the level of mental ingenuity. It requires a "baptism of the intelligence". This occurs because good theology is done in faith and under grace. But its human embodiment is, perhaps more than anything else, the persistence of a sense of wonder and the growth of humility before God's truth.

The things we admire and love most in children — the celebration of being, the native joie-de-vivre — may be global and primitive but they are certainly not negligible. They represent an obscure perception of both the goodness and the givenness of life. They involve both wonder and gratitude. Far from being autistic, to be grown out of, they constitute the foundations both of metaphysical awareness ("that things are") and of art (the celebration of being). It is no part of an educator's business to promote the disappearance of these qualities. His task is to nourish them.

The second factor that seems important, is the experience of dependence. Children feel helpless, vulnerable, at the mercy of others. Educators often see their task as leading children towards independence, towards autonomy. And of course we all want children to be able to stand on their own feet. Nevertheless, the experience of dependence does persist — which of us does not feel sometimes, that we are as flies to wanton boys. Moreover, it should persist, not as terror but as trust. According to E.H. Erikson, the first developmental crisis of childhood is that between trust and mistrust. Is "the other" basically trustworthy and loving? Or is it hostile or apathetic? In the latter case many think a strong strain of sadness is set up in the personality and an inability to form personal relationships grows. Is the world dependable, can we trust ourselves to it? Or are we to experience the growing fear of belonging "to another, or to others, or to God?"

In terms of these questions, dependence should be a permanent part of the human condition. This ability to trust and to belong is a part of that denial of our own self-sufficiency which is an essential element in the act of faith. If religion is a kind of strength it is also a kind of weakness. If it rejuvenates our life it hinges on a real acceptance of our own inadequacy.

A third quality is the capacity which children have for open and direct relationships which is why they often ask us such devastating personal questions. Often they can achieve relationships completely uncluttered by fear or convention. Again this quality of openness is one which lies among the roots of faith. While tact has to be learned

94

and the structure of social situations, we ought to cherish it rather than killing it off. Children then, will not have to go, as we do, to complicated and embarrassing sensitivity workshops in order to recover it.

These seem to be the characteristics of childhood which are of permanent and not of passing worth. They all lead forward and fit into a developmental scheme. None of them should cause a fixation at childishness either in human or in religious life. They are not, of course, overtly religious. They have no self-evident connection with the saving knowledge of Jesus Christ or the explicit word of gospel and Church. It is the task of the catechist in the early years of life to speak that word. His way of doing that should make the word of a piece with these crucial experiences of childhood. In that way a faith develops which is both of present value and full of promise for the future.